W9-BQL-543

Return of
Guatemala's Refugees

Photograph by Derrill Bazzy

Return of Guatemala's Refugees

Reweaving the Torn

Clark Taylor

Temple University Press *Philadelphia*

Temple University Press, Philadelphia 19122
Copyright © 1998 by Temple University.
All rights reserved
Published 1998
Printed in the United States of America

Text design by Dennis Anderson

⊗ The paper used in this publication meets the requirements of
American National Standard for Information Sciences—Permanence
of Paper for Printed Library Materials, ANSI z39.48–1984.

Library of Congress Cataloging-in-Publication Data
Taylor, Clark, 1934–
    Return of Guatemala's refugees : reweaving the torn / Clark Taylor.
        p.   cm.
    Includes bibliographical references and index.
    ISBN 1-56639-621-2 (alk. paper).—ISBN 1-56639-622-0 (pbk. : alk. paper)
      1. Return migration—Guatemala—Santa María Tzejá.   2. Santa María Tzejá
    (Guatemala)—History.   3. Refugees—Guatemala—Psychology.   4. Refugees—
    Mexico—Psychology.   5. Human rights—Guatemala.   6. Civil-military rela-
    tions—Guatemala.   7. Humanitarian assistance—Guatemala.   8. Assimilation
    (Sociology)   I. Title.
    JV416.T39   1998
    325′.27281—dc21   97-36545
                                                                            CIP

Frontispiece

The photo is of a *falda* (skirt) worn by an indigenous woman whose
community was torn apart by the Guatemalan army intent on wiping out
armed resistance forces that operated in her area. She lived with other
internally displaced people in what came to be known as Communities of
Population in Resistance (CPR's) until she was captured by the army in
1986. Her skirt bears evidence to the suffering she and others in the CPR's
endured in the years in which they sought to forge a brave freedom within
Guatemala.

This book is dedicated
to the
people of Santa María Tzejá—
pioneers in settling the Ixcán,
survivors of the scorched-earth violence of 1982,
and
reweavers of the torn.

Contents

Preface

With my wife, Kay, I am the co-leader of a project through which our local church has a partnership, ten years running as of the summer of 1997, with the Guatemalan village of Santa María Tzejá. Between us, we have accompanied twenty-one delegations to the village in twice-yearly visits. Although I teach Latin American studies at the University of Massachusetts in Boston, my primary focus in Santa María has never been research. But the combination of trusting friendships I have developed there and the importance of the story of the reintegrating of this community as a possible model for Guatemala leads me to write. That story, which I have come to know so well over the years, provides the case study material for this book. Members of the village community, when consulted in an open meeting in August 1996, reaffirmed through further consultation in June 1997, unanimously said that they wanted me to write this book so that their story could be more widely known.

The church–Santa María relationship has become a partnership between two communities. One partner is the Needham Congregational Church, a mainline Protestant church in suburban Boston of over seven hundred members belonging to the United Church of Christ denomination. The tie with Santa María is not with a church or parish as such but with the community as a whole, which has a population of 170 families or about a thousand people. One dimension of the relationship links 120 families in the Needham church with 120 families in the village and involves the exchange of letters every six months, in February and August, when delegations from the church visit the village. The church has made modest contributions of money to enable development projects defined by village leaders. Accountability is structured through written agreements and regular review of project management. But the primary thrust of the partnership is people to people, aimed at fostering solidarity. For the visitors to the village, that means, in part, taking increasing responsibility for understanding the impact of U.S. policy in the area and acting to do what we can to work for justice.

I first visited Santa María Tzejá in December 1985, in the company of an anthropologist who had visited the village years earlier. She was researching a book. Another man and I accompanied her for security purposes in the waning days of military dictatorship. We stayed in the community briefly. As we left she said, "Wouldn't it be great if there were international eyes on this village?" Her hope was to alert the world if the Guatemalan army struck out at the village and thus to offer its residents a measure of security. On my return to the United States, I proposed at the annual meeting of the church that we develop a partnership with the village, and a year later, in January 1987, we issued the invitation to Santa María to join us in finding out what such a partnership might involve.

That summer Kay and I made a brief visit and, with a handshake with the elected president of the village's development committee, set a tentative tie in motion. We brought our first delegations to visit in April and August 1988 and the next year established the February/August pattern that we have followed since. Nearly sixty individuals from the church have made the arduous journey, some of them several times. More than a third of the visitors have been high school and college young people, who have made vital contributions to the project. We have all been changed by the experience.

On one visit, Kay and I spent the month of July 1994 in Santa María, shortly after the return of a group of refugees from Mexico, where they had lived for twelve years. We divided our time between visits to the homes of returnees and of those who stayed in the village while the others were in Mexico. Other than a brief trip I had made in May 1994, at the time of the refugees' return, our summer visit was our introduction to the returnees. They had heard about our project while they were in Mexico, so they were disposed to greet us warmly, but that month-long visit enabled us to build trust with the whole community.

During a sabbatical in 1995–96, I spent several weeks in the village and did more formal interviews, with the thought that I might write this book. An additional trip in June 1997 provided updated material in the aftermath of the signing of the peace documents the previous December.

From the outset I want to acknowledge the people of Santa María Tzejá who continue to reweave their community and to contribute to the rebuilding of their nation. Their perseverence through unimaginable suffering and disruption, along with their good humor and creativity in putting their lives back together, have inspired this book.

Many individuals in a variety of settings and ways have enabled this project to proceed. Beatriz Manz, Curt Wands, Paula Worby, Randall Shea, Rachel Garst, Marcy Mersky, Dan Long, José Alberto (Padre Beto) Ghiglia, Benito Morales, Sr. Argentina Cuevas, Rolando Lopez, Grahame Russell, Brinton Lykes, Pat Goudvis, Margie Swedish, Alice Zachman, Angie Berryman, Lael Parish, Steve Bennett, Michael Willis, Gretta Tovar-Siebentritt, Jo-Ann Eccher, Micaela Morales, and Sunny Robinson have all been my friends and mentors. I want to give special thanks to Derrill Bazzy, Jonathan Moller, and Randall Shea for contributing their powerful photographs.

My colleagues at the College of Public and Community Service at the University of Massachusetts/Boston have been an important source of encouragement and critical insight. Three stand out for their help with the manuscript: Jim O'Brien, Vicky Steinitz, and Barry Phillips. Students in my courses on Guatemala have also challenged me in my analysis of the situation in the country.

Members of the Guatemala committee at the Needham Congregational Church have been my fellow travelers and support community for more than ten years as we worked out the partnership with Santa María Tzejá. Together we have struggled with challenging questions having to do with the engagement of peoples across space, culture, and class. The many contributions this group has made to the project have influenced the ideas in this book.

Finally, mention of partnership leads directly to my wife and life partner, Kay. In her roles as organizer of the letter project and as February delegation leader, she has come to understand the village in ways that have been very helpful to my analysis. In addition to all she does in organizing various aspects of the project, she is the first reader and critic of all I write, including *Return of Guatemala's Refugees*.

Introduction

ON FEBRUARY 13, 1982, the Guatemalan army stormed into the remote northern Guatemalan village of Santa María Tzejá. The inhabitants were gone. Given two hours' notice that the army was on the path to the village, and knowing that the army had destroyed other villages, residents had fled in terror. During the next five days, seventeen people from the village, nearly all women and children, were massacred, the animals slaughtered, and all the buildings burned to the ground. The external world learned nothing of the carnage.

Two days later, a village resident, Manuel Canil, was with his mother, wife, and six children, along with other members of their extended family. Thinking the family was safely hidden in a small ravine, he went with his older son to scout the location of a more sheltered location. Suddenly they heard gunfire in the area where the family was hidden. A dog had barked and alerted an army patrol, which killed nine people in the group. Manuel's youngest son, five at the time, managed to hide behind a bush. The others were machine-gunned; those still alive were executed with a shot to the head. Manuel's youngest daughter survived the initial shooting but was thrown in the air and bayonetted—according to her five-year-old brother, who saw it all. Manuel lost his mother, his wife, and four of his children.

Return of Guatemala's Refugees is about those Guatemalan peasants, and more than a million others like them. They are mostly indigenous Maya people who had the fabric of their lives torn apart by war and state-sponsored violence in the early 1980s. Hundreds of villages were razed and thousands of peasants slaughtered in a calculated scorched-earth drive by the army to eliminate an insurgent armed resistance.

It is impossible to imagine the terror of those people who were up-rooted from their homes. The majority of the displaced, estimated to be a million persons—more than a tenth of the population—stayed in Guatemala. Many found their way to urban areas, where they formed new squatter settlements. Some thirty thousand founded internal civilian resistance communities, where they lived clandestinely on constant guard, to stay out of reach of the army, which hunted them as an enemy. This latter group, known as the communities of population in resistance (CPRs), formed in three parts of the country, announcing their existence in 1990 and 1991. In the Ixcán, the CPRs came out in the open in 1993 in the hope that they could continue living together on some of the land they had occupied during their years living clandestinely.[1]

A substantial number of survivors—estimates range as high as two hundred thousand—fled to refuge in neighboring Mexico, where forty-six thousand were settled in official refugee camps—a number that rose, with births, to sixty thousand by the time of the returns.[2] The rest dispersed within the Mexican population. By the mid-1990s, more than thirty thousand refugees had returned to Guatemala, the majority in organized groups under terms spelled out in historic accords with the government, signed in October 1992.[3] As in any human movement, the returning refugees had a wide range of aspirations and plans. Some simply hoped to get a piece of land to provide for their families. But many had been exposed to education in human rights and grassroots democracy, had successful experience organizing for the return, and planned to work for deep-rooted change when they returned. Together, the returnees represented an out-of-control threat to the army's ongoing effort to pacify and control the population.

"Reweaving the torn" was the unavoidable work facing both the returning refugees and those who had stayed in Guatemala. The fabric of their lives had been ripped apart, and now, if the country was ever going to heal itself, they had to reweave, thread by thread, re-creating patterns as best they could. In some cases, as in Santa María Tzejá, that reweaving involved renewing relationships between original members of the same community. In other cases, new communities had to be formed between returnees and people in Guatemala who had never known each other before the violence. But everywhere the process was between peoples who had had profoundly contrasting experiences on the two sides of the Mexican-Guatemalan border.

The process of reweaving was complicated because the army had brought in people friendly to it to take over land vacated by those who fled to become refugees. These *nuevos* (new ones or newcomers), as they were known, were poor, often landless peasants themselves, who were delighted to get land they were told would be theirs forever. Very understandably, they resisted the return of the refugees to their original lands (Manz 1988a, chap. 5).

Likewise, the process was complicated by the relationship of the returnees with the armed resistance, known as the URNG (Guatemalan National Revolutionary Unity), a coalition of four rebel groups. In its fight against the injustices of the military dictatorship that ruled Guatemala, the URNG had worked closely with the population the army attacked in the early 1980s. Many of those who fled to Mexico had ties with the insurgency and maintained strategic alliances with one or another of the rebel groups during the years in refuge. The refugees, however, were a civilian population and acted in that role as they planned and carried out their return. They shared a similar perspective with the guerrillas but were not dominated by them (NCOORD newsletter, 1996, 2–3).

Back in Guatemala, the returnees both posed and faced critical challenges. Those challenges are the subject of this book. Although they constituted a diverse group, from the army's perspective they had been "infected" by contact with the guerrillas, by human rights training, and by successful experience in organizing. They could not be counted on to fit into the army's control system. In fact, their leaders had shown great skill in organizing the return process, negotiating conditions for the return, and heading an initial triumphal procession through the capital. Given all this and the presence of international observers, the army's options were limited; violent repression would be difficult to carry out with the world watching. As potential organizers of the country's repressed majority, the returnees were a threat to the army's domination. But with their demands for land and a fair piece of the economic pie, they posed an indirect challenge as well to the country's economic system, which delivers inordinate wealth to a narrow elite while some 80 percent of the population struggles in poverty.[4]

At the same time, the returnees faced the challenge of maintaining their own integrity and momentum in the face of counterpressures and internal issues. Many had been fired with a new sense of themselves as bearers of human rights, which included a determination to resist army control. But their human rights training had not been tested in the Guatemalan arena, where the army was intent on maintaining control. Further, the refugee population was far from united internally as it crossed the border. So their new learning and their aspirations for a just, democratic society faced severe pressure as the return process followed its course.

As the refugees prepared to return, they negotiated with the Guatemalan government to ensure that conditions would exist to support their reentry and reintegration. They wanted to be sure they could move about freely and not be subject to military control. They wanted assurances that they would have access to land. But they also demanded guarantees that internationals could accompany and live with them to be witnesses, eyes and ears, to ensure the world would know if the government and army went back on their word.

The purpose of this book is to spotlight the refugees' return, to analyze its impact at a critical juncture in Guatemalan history, and to enlist reader involvement. A thirty-six-year civil war was formally concluded on December 29, 1996, but the underlying issues of the unjust distribution of land, wealth, and political power were left unresolved. Yet with the signing of the peace accords, the world was led to believe that the Guatemalan "problem" was solved. That was an enormous misperception. The reality was that a new era in the struggle for a just society in Guatemala had just begun. Every word in the peace accords has become contested political territory, with the elites, fully supported by international allies, having the initial advantage. The hope for building a people-centered democratic system depends on the poor majority forging as much unity as possible among grassroots organizations to maximize its voice and political leverage. That, in turn, will require international solidarity and assistance now and for the long haul.

This book highlights the experiences of the people of Santa María Tzejá, the village struck by the violence described in the opening paragraphs of this introduction. The successful return of these villagers is a key to Guatemala's future because it is a microcosm of the struggle of poor and marginalized peoples for integral development, human rights, and grassroots democracy in that country. It is a microcosm, furthermore, in which the issues of the reintegration of returnees and those who stayed were being played out within a population of people who were all original settlers of this community. This was one village, torn in half by the violence, where the two halves—minus those who died and plus the many who were born in the interim—are now physically back together. Unlike many other returns, in which the returnees hailed from different locations, in Santa María the issues of separation and reintegration can be understood in their "purest" form, as one community torn and coming together. In that relatively "controlled" sense, the village's experience of re-weaving the torn provides a lens through which the precise impact of leaving for refuge in Mexico and staying under the power of the Guatemalan army can be seen most clearly in the reintegration process.

The drama being played out in Santa María has wider implications. To the extent that the village continues successfully on its path of reintegration, it expands the reach of democracy and human rights in its immediate region and, indirectly, throughout the country. In that process, as its success becomes known, the village can become a reference point and model for communities in other countries. An important objective, in a world increasingly dominated by transnational corporations, is to connect people from different countries who are building democracy from the ground up.

Creating effective grassroots democracy will continue to depend on the initiative of people like those in Santa María. If they are to succeed, however, they must have the active support of people in the developed world who will work with them in specific roles: first, as friends and human rights observers; second, as a force organizing politically to bring external pressure on the Guatemalan government to support the democratic aspirations of its people; and, third, as a lobbying group working to change policy in the United States and Canada to free Guatemala, and countries in its region, from "client status" to the industrial powers to the north.

The Village in Context

Santa María Tzejá was one of scores of villages founded and developed in the late 1960s and throughout the 1970s in the remote northern rainforest area of Guatemala known as the Ixcán. Land reform, in the sense of redistributing land already under cultivation, was anathema to the country's reigning oligarchy. But a conviction took hold that it would be useful for the country to relieve some of the pent-up pressure for land by allowing campesinos (peasants) to colonize the rainforest. A plan, supported by the National Institute for Agrarian Transformation (INTA), was organized to survey and parcel out land in the region (Manz 1988b, 73).

The original impetus for the establishment of Santa María was an invitation by a Spanish Catholic priest, Luis Gurriarán (Padre Luis), to a group of campesinos to explore options for founding a new community. They were drawn from several communities in the department (political province/state) of Quiché. They identified land that was pure jungle at the time and set about the herculean task of clearing it for housing and agriculture. The majority of the original settlers, 115 families, were K'iche'-speaking Maya people, but there were also nine ladino families (mestizos who spoke only Spanish) among the early settlers (Gurriarán 1993).

The composition of the village was thus overwhelmingly Maya in origin, although many indigenous traditions atrophied as the relocated population adapted to new circumstances. Coming, as they did, from several traditional communities, the Santa María residents left behind the festivals and uniqueness of their particular villages of origin. As Catholics, and organized by a Catholic priest, they were removed from their Maya religious roots, which loosened their ties to traditional medicinal use as well. At the same time, their centuries-long involvement with the soil and the raising of corn and other basic foods to feed their families was strengthened with their acquisition of adequate land. And they continued to speak K'iche', an anchor of their culture, in their homes.

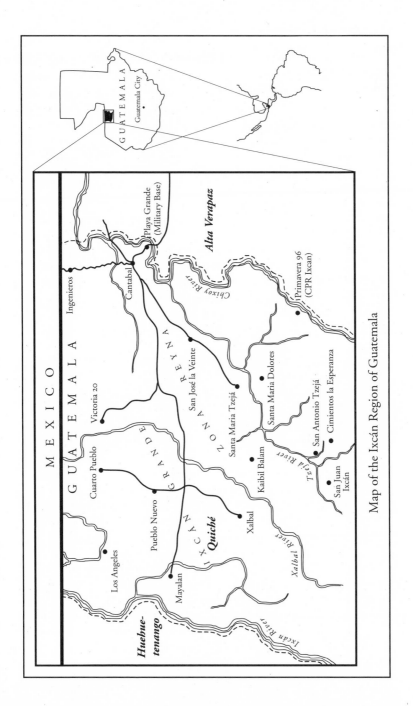

Map of the Ixcán Region of Guatemala

The first exploratory probes toward relocation to what would become Santa María took place in the late 1960s, but the army barred initial settlement for a time because of an incipient guerrilla movement in the area. Work teams began the arduous work of carving the community out of the jungle in 1970 and started bringing their families a year later. Antecedents of what would become open warfare in the area were evident from the beginning as residents found themselves in territory contested by insurgents and the army (Gurriarán 1993).[5]

Women had their own experience in the forming of the community. Initially, many of them resisted joining their husbands, recognizing how nearly impossible it would be to raise their children in the jungle. On arrival, the families faced hunger and a lack of replacement clothing, as what they wore on arrival turned to rags. Wild animals killed the few domestic animals they had for food. Sickness was a constant struggle in the hot, mosquito-infested lowland area, a sharp contrast to the cooler climate of their former highland homes.

Community development did take root, however, to an extent that village residents were able to plant what they needed to eat and have some left to sell. Corn, the central food of the Maya diet and way of life, would be the main crop, but the market for sale of the corn would be very limited. Cardamom, a spice used in Middle Eastern and Asian countries, was introduced as a successful cash crop. Padre Luis led the settlers to form a cooperative to buy supplies and sell their products. With help from the international Heifer Foundation, each member of the cooperative was able to acquire and raise several head of cattle. In spite of pressures in the area, the community was beginning to thrive and momentum was high.

But storm clouds of the civil war settled into the area. Death threats and actual assassinations of community workers tore at the villagers' sense of well-being and hope. Raisa, a dedicated young schoolteacher, was the first to be killed by paramilitary forces supporting the government, in January 1976. Over the next five years, eight other community workers—outsiders who lived together and served the village—were killed. In September 1976, Padre Luis was forced to flee the country, following a series of threats, so that his presence would not continue to endanger the people he worked with

(Manz 1988b, 76–77). In 1978, when General Lucas García came to power, savage violence was unleashed in the country, culminating in the early 1980s with a genocidal scorched-earth campaign calculated to deprive the guerrillas of support by depopulating the Ixcán (Handy 1984, chap. 8).

The Return to Santa María

The refugees who returned to Santa María Tzejá in May 1994 were part of a series of organized, collective, and voluntary returns carried out under the provisions of a formal agreement signed on October 8, 1992, between the Guatemalan government and refugee representatives. Prior to that agreement, in spite of government efforts to lure the refugees back, only eighty-six hundred had responded. Once back, they were inserted into highly militarized villages and treated with suspicion by the authorities. The repatriates were required to sign an *amnistía*, by which they admitted, in effect, that they had left for subversive reasons (Rader 1997, 42; Ghiglia 1997, 22). As used in the context of Guatemala, the term "repatriation" carries a different meaning than the term "return":

> The term "repatriation" is the internationally accepted term for those being returned to their country. In the Guatemalan context these individuals, groups or families go back under individual agreements between the Mexican and Guatemalan governments and facilitated by the UNHCR. Those who "return," in the Guatemalan context, are those who go back under the October 8, 1992 Accord, signed by refugee representatives and the Guatemalan government. This allows for a "voluntary, collective and organized" return. Under this accord, "returnees" are eligible for land, financial credit and other benefits (NCOORD 1997, 15).

In 1988, eight families returned to Santa María as repatriates. One informant in that group regularly reported the difficulties they had in rebuilding their lives. According to the informant, they were regarded with suspicion and had to be constantly on guard, particularly in the first years after their return.[6]

Following the October 1992 accords, the first of the returns crossed the border on January 20, 1993. Seventy buses brought two thousand returnees to a tumultuous welcome at the border and, a few days later, in Guatemala City. From 1993 to 1996, a continuous series of returns brought more than 17,800 refugees back to Guatemala. They were, for the most part, highly organized and committed to changing their country:

> In contrast to those who had repatriated to the Ixcán before 1993, those organized into collective returns went home to Guatemala aware that their political skills and unity would be a positive force: not only for the resolution of their own claims for land and assistance, but rather for a general movement to force the government to support economic development, a respect for human rights and demilitarization for the Ixcán and all of Guatemala. A slogan, often shouted in Mexico as refugees organized to return home, became a rallying point once they crossed the border: "¡Luchar para retornar! ¡Retornar para luchar!" ("Struggle to Return! Return to Struggle!") (Rader 1997, 43).

Cesar Díaz, director of the development agency Alianza, described the substantial impact of the return movement following the 1992 accords. He said that the returns opened the eyes of the population of Guatemala in general to the possibilities that citizens could demand their rights and win important changes in response. But, he added, the return process took place in a context that was highly influenced by a counterinsurgency mindset and an "addiction to national security." The collective force of the obstacles thrown in the path of the return movement, including lack of follow-through on provisions of the accords, had the effect of dividing the returnees and reducing their impact on the society (interview, June 1997).

In spite of that reduced momentum, however, Diaz maintained that the returnee movement had had a major political impact on the country. Among other important gains, it had enabled some Guatemalans, including those in Santa María, to recover land they held before the violence and others to acquire land for the first time. Dan Long, the World Council of Churches' representative in Guatemala and a member of the negotiating team working on return issues, agreed. While noting the myriad difficulties returnees have faced and the divisions that have developed in some of their communities, he argued that the new ideas and organizational skills they brought back have made them a motor for change in the country (interview, June 1997).

The actual number of refugees who returned under the 1992 accord was quite small: 3,747 in 1993, 4,123 in 1994, 7,018 in 1995, and 2,919 in 1996 (NCOORD 1997, 15). But the fact that the returnees were guaranteed land and credit under the accord made them a particular kind of problem for the government, which had to identify and negotiate land purchases. In addition, that the returnees knew their rights and had experience appealing to national and international media gave them additional force.

Taken as a whole, then, the return movement has been a major challenge for the governing authorities, including the army—and the returnees, in turn, have faced monumental challenges. The returnees' slogan was "Return to Struggle!" The struggle was on.

Overview of the Book

To understand the dynamics of the villagers' return, one needs to understand the terror unleashed in the early 1980s when the Guatemalan system felt it was threatened. Chapter 1 details these events in Santa María Tzejá. In six terrible days in February 1982 and thereafter for months, the community was sundered and many family members were lost to each other for years. This experience begs the question, which will be explored in chapter 1, "Why would a national army turn so savagely on its own people?"

Chapter 2 analyzes what happened to two groups of people with dramatically different experiences: those who spent twelve years in Mexico, away from the Guatemalan army, and those who had to accommodate themselves to that army, now bent on total control, in their homeland. Having come from the same language group and having experienced the intense process of building Santa María, the two groups developed distinct subcultures in the years of separation, one based in fear and the other in a framework of learning about human rights and organizing for the return.

Those subcultures eventually came together in local areas throughout rural Guatemala, in a dynamic national context. That context is described in Chapter 3. A major dimension of the national picture was the slow but ultimately successful effort to end the country's thirty-six-year civil war, culminating in the December 1996 signing of the "Firm and Lasting Peace." Not only does Chapter 3 describe the steps of the peace process, it also analyzes the relative strengths of Guatemala's grassroots groups and powerful sectors, the major protagonists in the struggle to implement the peace accords and define Guatemala's identity in the years ahead. A central purpose of the chapter is to provide an analytic framework for assessing changes that affect the whole country but particularly the rural areas that are the focal point of the book.

The heart of the book is an analysis of five profound challenges posed and faced by returning refugees and the receiving population. As in the first two chapters, case study material is drawn from the experience of Santa María Tzejá. Successful assimilation served to increase the level of threat the returnees represented to the army and economic elites. But likewise, success in meeting the challenges meant stronger support for human rights and grassroots democracy. To the extent that the returnees were diverted from, or divided by, these challenges, they became less of a threat and less effective in contributing to a people-responsive democracy.

Chapter 4 examines the first challenge facing the returnees—integrating the subculture of fear generated among those who stayed in Guatemala with the human rights–focused subculture stimulated in the population who fled to Mexico. A careful analysis reveals the depth of the differences to be overcome. The categories of differences between the two groups provide some guidelines for thinking about and addressing these differences in other settings.

Chapter 5 addresses the fascinating question of whether the flood of international money given by Canada, European governments, and others was a bane or a blessing in the reweaving process. Answering this question leads to the further question "Development of what and for whom?" The challenge is to develop communities with integrity that springs from the vision, plans, and initiative of the people themselves.

Where the role of human rights is in the background in Chapters 1 through 5, Chapter 6 focuses on the way the challenge of creating a culture supportive of human rights is at the heart of expanding the space for grassroots democracy in Guatemala.

Chapter 7 takes up the fourth challenge, which for the returnees and for those who stayed is coming to grips with the unresolved grief and trauma rooted in the violence of the early 1980s.

Chapter 8 analyzes the ultimate challenge faced by the return-ees—how to deal with the army, that is, how to reintegrate and build grassroots democracy under conditions of extreme poverty, in which the privileged still have to rely on some form of repression to contain the potential for social explosion. The army is publicly changing its image to conform to the requirements of the peace accords. But given the vast inequalities of resources between rich and poor, the threat and practice of physical and economic repression will continue in some form. The question, then, is how the returnees and their allies can manage the political space in a way that will allow progres-sive change to develop from the base.

Chapter 9, the final chapter, assesses the impact of the refugee return movement and makes recommendations keyed to ensuring successful returns. It then considers what needs to be done in soli-darity with people working for justice in Guatemala. Six forms of response are outlined, including education, witnessing, accompani-ment, advocacy, direct nonviolent action, and national movement building, along with specific suggestions for how to proceed at each point.

Guatemala challenges our humanity. This small Central American country is a microcosm of U.S. and other "First World" policy in the Third World. To protect U.S. corporate power and profits, the Eisenhower administration crushed the only democratic government the people of Guatemala had ever known. The United States then trained and equipped what has become, in the Guatemalan army, one of the most brutally repressive forces in the Western Hemi-sphere. Now, as returnees and people who stayed attempt to reweave what was torn from them in the early 1980s—and as the country as a whole seeks to weave a new social fabric (there is no sense at that level of *re*weaving what was never an integrated pattern)—the role of the United States is once again up for criticism and action.

As in Guatemala, groups with grassroots and corporate interests in the United States and in other developed nations will contest what foreign policy should be for Guatemala and its region. Corporate interests have a clear agenda: in the name of "free trade" to maintain countries like Guatemala as providers of commodities and cheap labor for textile and other manufacturing. Those who stand with the people of Guatemala at the grassroots level must develop an equally clear agenda and plan of action. This book seeks to point the way.

CHAPTER ONE

Torn by Terror

My eyes have seen what no human eyes should see.

—Oldest man in Santa María Tzejá

I N A 1990 briefing for a visiting delegation, an army spokes-
man pointed to a map of Guatemala in which a substan-
tial part of the national territory was shaded in red. He indicated that
the shaded area had come under guerrilla influence or control in 1981.
The communist threat, in his ideological framework, was very real
and determined to take power. The government, under military dictatorship at the time, decided to do whatever was necessary to regain
total control, to dominate the people so completely that they could
never rise up again.[1]

Former army general Benedicto Lucas claimed that in 1982 the
military thought the guerrillas were within fifteen days of taking
power. Lucas, accused of directing the most heinous of war crimes
against the civilian population, defended what had been done as necessary to save the state during that chaotic and desperate time. His
summary words were that "sadly, peace and tranquility come to a
country after the spilling of blood."[2]

So the Guatemalan army, determined to eliminate the armed resistance, set out to butcher and terrorize. There would be no mercy.
The sheer magnitude of its savagery staggers belief. By the army's
own count, 440 villages were destroyed. Tens of thousands of human
beings, mostly Maya civilian campesinos, were slaughtered.[3]

Scorched Earth: Terror and Burning

The people living in the villages in the army's path had no way of
anticipating how brutal the destruction would be. Many simply

refused to believe the army would destroy them. One witness, referring to a nearby community, said, "We knew they killed a lot of people there, but we didn't think it would happen here" (Falla 1994, 62).

The year 1982 was designated by the army as "Victory 82" in its long-range military campaign. The objective was to pacify the country and reorganize the population to serve the purposes of its counterinsurgency effort. The following year was labeled "Firmness '83," when a pacified nation was to be "developed" under the stern hand of the military—characterized by a "beans and bullets" theme: "You work with us and we feed you; you carry guns under our orders to fight the subversives." Likewise, each of the next several years was referred to as a stage in the return to civilian government within a militarized framework.[4]

The scorched-earth campaign was not the result of blind, impetuous fury but part of a deliberate, rational plan laid out by military men to master the civil population. These men felt they needed to tear the fabric of their own nation, the *patria*, in order to reweave it according to their own pattern. The lengths to which they were willing to go is on the record:

> To those who have studied [the army's "Guatemala solution"] in detail on the basis of interviews and primary documents, what is most striking is the unity and single-minded determination of all those involved in the campaign against *la subversión*. Inherent within this vision was the assumption that the planned genocide that left 100 – 150,000 civilian casualties was necessary to establish "social peace"; the human rights crimes were simply beside the point, because the Indian population was "subversive" by definition (Jonas 1991, 148).

According to Ricardo Falla, a Guatemalan priest and anthropologist who chronicled the massacres, "The offensive advanced geographically, according to the counterinsurgency manuals, like a huge broom sweeping from the more populated areas to the more remote areas" (1994, 60). The objective was to eliminate the enemy by depopulating the indigenous peasants who had recently settled in the Ixcán region.

The army's tactic was to enter a village on a weekend, when residents would be gathered in the center trading area. In his careful style, never reaching beyond the evidence for which he had multiple sources, Falla tells us what happened in early 1982:

> On the weekend of 13 February, the army carried out massacres that resulted in the killings of between 12 and 17 people in Santa María Tzejá, between 27 and 41 in Santo Tomás and about 15 in San Lucas, and 7 on the road to San Lucas. On 18 February (not on a weekend, so presumably not part of the plan), the army massacred 10 people. On the weekend of 20 February, it massacred 13 persons in Polígono 14, and on the weekend of 27 February, the army went to Kaibil Balam, killing 12 to 14 people (1994, 53).

Falla here records the deaths in the first two weeks of a campaign that would last for months. He notes only those caught in the direct path of the army dreadnought. He says nothing of the thousands who fled in terror into the jungle, most with only the clothes on their backs. At other points, Falla names villages where the entire population was slaughtered.

The depth of the depravity is revealed in Falla's description of the use of torture:

> Systematic torture was integral to every level of repression. Sometimes obtaining information from the victim was emphasized and sometimes the torture was aimed at terrorizing others. Terror may have two objectives: to inhibit all activity against the army and to force people to provide information. I have found evidence of individual torture, by well-known methods (burning with firebrands, submerging in water, asphyxiating), and also of collective torture. I believe that burning people alive, a practice documented so often in this book, can be considered collective torture. . . . The depths of savagery are symbolized by the places of torture and death: pits in the military outposts, tunnels where prisoners were held, the room in the military barracks in Santa Cruz del Quiché that was thickly coated in clotted blood, and the crematorium of freshly butchered bodies in Playa Grande (1994, 184).

This tearing of the social fabric of Guatemala was, thus, deliberate, systematic, and relentless on the part of the army. Its purpose was to break the will to resist, to render a proud people pliant and submissive. The full brunt of the terror—the burning and the slaughter—hit Santa María Tzejá on Saturday, February 13, 1982.

Terror in Santa María Tzejá

The oldest man in Santa María Tzejá fled with his family to their parcel of land, not far from the town center, where they could hear their animals being killed and see the smoke rising from their burning homes. Later he recalled, "My eyes have seen," he said, "what no human eyes should see."[5]

Another man told how his family had a new baby, just seven days old, on the thirteenth of February. The army arrived at their part of town at about two in the afternoon. Because they lived some distance from the center, they weren't aware of what was happening. When the army came near, they escaped, with only the clothes on their backs. Their house, all their food, and their animals were destroyed. They were left cowering in their cornfields, not knowing what was happening beyond their cornfields or why. They lived in isolated dread for periods ranging from two weeks to a year and a half, fearing that they would be tortured and murdered at any moment.

Manuel Canil, whose mother, wife, and four children were murdered, reported that on Wednesday, February 10, all but two villagers in nearby La Trinitaria were massacred. One survivor found the way to Santa María, where he told what had happened. Then, on Saturday, the thirteenth, men were working in their fields near the neighboring village of San José la Veinte when they saw columns of smoke rising from the direction of that village and figured it had been torched and the army would be coming to Santa María. Word of the army on the path came shortly, and all in Santa María grabbed what they could; some buried their most precious possessions and fled on foot for a half-hour to an hour and a half to their farmlands. In the melee family members were separated, in some cases for the next twelve years.

Manuel recalled feeling stunned as he realized what had happened. He tried to absorb the unspeakable loss of his mother, his wife, and four of his children. Amid the awful loneliness of that moment, he called to mind Jesus's words from the cross, "My God, my God, why have you forsaken me?"

Thirty-five long days later, he and other relatives returned to the site of the massacre. In a frenzy of agitation, they buried their relatives' remains in a shallow grave, all the while fearing that the army would discover and kill those who had returned.[6]

Manuel's thirteen-year-old niece, the daughter of his brother Pedro and his wife, Juana, was among those murdered. The event is reported as part of a powerful play, *The Past Is with Us*, about that terrible time in Santa María. It was written by Randall Shea, a U.S. citizen living and teaching in the village during that period. The scene in which Pedro's daughter is killed is told through the words of the girl's mother:

> We had to move quickly. My eldest daughter, María Isabel, wanted to carry her little sister. I told her, No! It's better if I take her! Run, go! María took off running. A short while later, I heard the burst of gunfire. Ay, who knows who they are killing now?! When my husband told me they had killed María Isabel (falling to her knees), I thought I was going to die. I wanted to cry. I wanted to scream!! (rising) Even today I still wonder, I still ask myself, if I had allowed María Isabel to carry her little sister, perhaps she would have stayed at my side; perhaps she'd still be alive today. But I told her no, and perhaps that's what caused her to die. I don't know. Only God knows.

Why the Army Turned on Its People

As in all the villages that the army attacked, the people of Santa María Tzejá experienced stunned disbelief at the merciless violence directed against them. Santa María residents had heard enough about nearby destruction and killing to know they had to flee when they heard the army was on the path toward their village. But they had no answer to the question of why the army treated the villagers so cruelly. Falla describes how the people of the nearby village of Cuarto Pueblo refused to believe the army would destroy their town and didn't flee. On the Sunday the army sweep reached Cuarto Pueblo and in the three days following, 324 people were massacred (1994, 102).

To understand why the army would destroy Santa María, Cuarto Pueblo, and hundreds of other villages requires one to examine a much larger time period and territory than Guatemala in the 1970s and 1980s. The analysis starts with the Spanish conquest in the

1520s, when land use and political patterns were set for the over-whelming benefit of the Spanish invaders. Guatemala was part of a region that separated from the Spanish empire in the 1820s, but as Gabriel Aguilera Peralta, a Guatemalan political scientist, points out, the Guatemalan army did not arise from any glorious history:

> The circumstances in which the country's armed forces were born ex-plain some of the aspects of its present ideology. There was not a pe-riod of heroic struggle for independence from Spain in which a mili-tary group was created. Rather, the army was created to collaborate with the national program of coffee growers, which implied a system of domination based on repression (1983, 115).

Aguilera Peralta then analyzes the development of the Guatemalan economy, as a prelude to examining the power of the army. The econ-omy, he argues, served the interest of transnational capital. In the nineteenth century, the economy depended on the sale of coffee, but it later diversified to include bananas, cotton, and sugar. A distin-guishing characteristic of this owning class, even as it expanded into the industrial, commercial, and financial sectors, was its lack of po-litical legitimacy (Aguilera Peralta 1983, 117).

Susanne Jonas develops the same point regarding the relationship of Guatemala's economic elites to foreign capital but also suggests that its influence was to isolate the owners even further from the in-terests of the majority of the people:

> The influx of foreign capital (primarily U.S.-based multinational cor-porate investment in industry) also reinforced the intransigence of the Guatemalan bourgeoisie. While introducing new technologies, and in this sense "modernizing" Guatemalan capitalism, foreign interests shared the absolute opposition to any redistributive reforms and the generally right-wing political perspective (1991, 89).

Jonas concurs on the question of legitimacy, noting that the bour-geoisie did not administer state power directly because it had no le-gitimacy beyond itself, no popular following. So it worked through what she terms a "ruling coalition," which included, most notably, the army but also bureaucrats, professionals, and the "political class" (1991, 92).

The modern formation of the Guatemalan army took shape un-der U.S. tutelage, following the Eisenhower administration's CIA-managed overthrow of the democratic government headed by Jacobo Arbenz in 1954. President Arbenz and his predecessor, President Juan José Arévalo, administered a brief democratic period from 1944 to 1954 that fostered a free press, union organizing, and land reform. While the declared justification for the overthrow was to stop the spread of communism in the hemisphere, the reality was that a U.S. "gunboat" effort was under way to protect the Boston-based United Fruit Company from having any of its idle land expropriated for an Arbenz-initiated land-redistribution program. That story is detailed in a number of excellent sources.[7]

Following the overthrow, dubbed "Operation Success" by the Eisenhower administration, the United States installed as president a pliable army officer, Colonel Castillo Armas. In the aftermath, the achievements of the democratic years were reversed and a wave of violent repression unleashed. In response, an armed insurgency, with roots in an aborted army rebellion in 1960, began to be organized among the rural population. The United States, with a high stake in preserving its "democracy project," provided military aid to the Guatemalan army, along with training in counterinsurgency strategy. An important element of the latter was the introduction in the mid-1960s of the use of state terrorism:

> United States counter-insurgency doctrine encouraged the Guatema-lan military to adopt both new organizational forms and new tech-niques in order to root out insurgency more effectively. New techniques would revolve around a central precept of the new counter-insurgency: that counter insurgent war must be waged free of restriction by laws, by the rules of war, or moral considerations: guerilla "terror" could be defeated only by the untrammelled use of "counter-terror," the terror-ism of the state.[8]

Foot soldiers in Guatemala's army were press-ganged into service. Military trucks would descend on buses, marketplaces, movie thea-ters—wherever young men might be gathered—and simply round up recruits. Those with enough money could bribe their way out. The rest, who tended to be indigenous and poor, had no options. Their training was brutal, and they were set against their own people:

> Conscript training is a process of indoctrination in anti-communism and systematic brutalization; in interviews, former conscripts have de-

scribed sessions in which recruits are obliged to submit to regular beatings and treatment that could accurately be described as torture. Maltreatment is ordered as part of a toughening and desensitizing process, with members of the same training units alternating in giving and receiving physical punishment. Discipline is enforced and instilled by physical punishment. . . . [One recruit, when] asked whether he would have killed his father, his mother, or his sister, said he would kill "anyone who turned up, if we were ordered to" (McClintock 1985, 165).

Thus, the army had a history of serving the interests of the economic elites. Then, following the overthrow of the Arbenz government, the army was trained by U.S. military advisers in counterterrorism and its foot soldiers were brutalized to the point of being ready to kill their own families if they were told to do it.

The trigger for the decision to resort to unlimited savagery was the surging momentum of the guerrilla forces in 1980–81. Military and economic elites faced the possibility that the government could be overthrown. The specter of the Nicaraguan revolution of 1979, in which the Somoza dictatorship had been overturned, was fresh in their minds. The army was ready, and the decision was made to unleash the terror.

Top military officers and their allies had a defense grounded in Latin American history and culture. They were charged to defend the fatherland, the patria, from all threats (Loveman 1998, chap. 2). In the context of the Cold War, fueled by the ideological energy of the key leaders of the Western Alliance, including Presidents Truman, Eisenhower, Kennedy, Nixon, and Ford, the Guatemalan military had a mission to turn back all hints of "atheistic communism" in the name of Christianity and Western values. In that framework the guerrillas became the "needed enemy" by embracing the notion that the elites would never cede power voluntarily and that the oppressed poor would have to organize to seize it.

North American readers are conditioned by the public media and the prevailing ideology to think of guerrillas-as-communists-as-bad. There is a tendency to think, "The army may have overdone it, but it had to get rid of the communists." The guerrillas, however, were not the root problem; they were the *presenting* problem and the immediate target for the army. A compelling poster has it right: "It isn't the rebels who cause the troubles of the world; it's the troubles that cause the rebels." The brutal injustice and repression meted out by the ruling elite gave the poor reason to support the guerrillas, who promised to deliver justice if they were victorious.

Far from responding to the historically legitimate land claims and other rights of the indigenous population, the government, oligarchy, and military, in collaboration with their U.S. allies, had continuously seized land illegally simply because they had the greedy desire and the power to do it. In 1944, when the people overthrew a dictatorship and elected a democratic government that attempted to right some of the wrongs, that government was an aberration to the elites that had to be overthrown. The United States, which might have been a brake on the process of repression had it followed its own publicly stated values, was itself an agent in the repression.

The answer, then, to the question of why the Guatemalan army turned so savagely on its people is woven through the history of the country. And, once it embarked on a path of protecting the resources of the country for the interests of the few—including by now the top officers in the army, who had enriched themselves through the spoils of war—there was no turning back. Had the army and its allies held back at the point of the serious guerrilla threat, officers in the army and its supporters would have not only been defeated but faced charges for the atrocities they had already committed. In the docket, they would have heard how horribly wrong it was to overthrow a democratic government and take land from the poor, to kill the leaders of grassroots movements, and to burn villages and kill tens of thousands of civilians. To admit error at that point would have been to admit to heinous crimes against humanity. They could not do it. The guilty had too much blood on their hands.[9]

Months of Hell

The unspeakable horror that occurred in Santa María Tzejá on the thirteenth of February gave way to days, weeks, and then months of hiding. A few villagers left fairly quickly for Mexico. But most fled to their cornfields, where they waited in isolated terror. Who could imagine the army would continue to threaten and kill indefinitely?

Surely it would leave after a time. Gradually, however, it became clear that life was changed forever.

Most fled with only the clothes on their backs. They faced disease, especially malaria, with no medicine. Storms lashed at them. Babies were born, and some died. Families constantly struggled to find food, and what they found could be cooked only during darkness, so the smoke would not give away their hiding places.[10]

A man described the fear they experienced:

> We were always very afraid, because at that time, if they thought a family was hiding out in their *parcela*, the army would come to look for them from a helicopter. When a helicopter passed over, we hid. We couldn't cook during the day, only very early in the morning, from three to four. . . . The most serious sickness we faced was the mental illness of my mother, who couldn't sleep at all for three months. That was the saddest kind of sickness we experienced (interview, June 1997).

One family fled with six children, including two very young ones. They spent eight months in their cornfields, where they ate grass and roots to stay alive. Whenever the army found food, they burned it— "so we would die."

Another man described how his twelve-year-old daughter has chronic nervousness and recurrent ear infections, the results, the family believes, of the conditions of her earliest months, when her family was in hiding. In another home a man related how his family and his brother's family found each other after the initial massacre but that his brother was shot at and captured by the army a few weeks later. They would not see each other for eleven years. He learned on his return that his brother had been tortured for several months before being allowed to return to his land. Another man pointed to a cave on his land where fifteen families hid for three months, hoping the army wouldn't find them.

Some villagers, as they fled, kept reliving the unbearable pain of having loved ones torn from them before their eyes. All had to survive like animals on corn left from earlier harvests, roots, wild fruits, and fear.

In a few villages the entire population was slaughtered, but in the rest villagers recalled similar experiences of flight, sickness, death, and living beyond the level of anyone's worst imaginings. A woman from one village vividly described how she was captured by the army but escaped into a rainy night, her chains still on her arms, when her guard fell asleep. For thousands of people whose security and sense of place was destroyed, each day was unending trauma.

Survival Options

Individuals and family groups gradually found each other and discussed what they could do, given that the army was still firmly in control of the village area. Various survival strategies surfaced as the months unfolded. Three distinct lines of action can be noted here. Some decided to leave for Mexico, a few very quickly and others after several months, once they realized how long the army was going to remain in the village. Others were either captured or gave themselves up and just over a year later were allowed to form the core of the repopulation of Santa María. Still others became part of the internally displaced, either by finding their way to the capital or other urban centers or by becoming part of communities of population in resistance. The latter lived within the Guatemalan national territory in remote areas as a civil population, in a symbiotic relation with the guerrillas but away from the control of the army.

Santa María's population divided roughly evenly between those who found their way to Mexico and those who for one reason or another found themselves back in the village within a year or so. Two families became part of the CPRs, and a few people dispersed to other parts of Guatemala.

A family that later took refuge in Mexico at first hid alone in its cornfields but gradually made contact with others. By the time the group decided to leave for Mexico, there were more than ninety people. Single young men served as scouts at the front and back of the group, while families with small children stayed in the middle. The scouts followed the movements of the army, identifying what seemed like the safest route. At one point one hundred soldiers passed close by. The storyteller laughed as he described the incident, but clearly it was a terrifying moment. Crossing the river at the border was another trial. Fortunately, they attracted the attention of

Mexicans with boats, who picked them up and delivered them to the other side.

Once in Mexico, the Guatemalans were greeted with open arms by the indigenous campesinos who lived in the Lacondon Forest area of Chiapas, and there the refugees found a safe space to build their lives. They soon organized in camps, largely by Maya ethnic/language groups.

The refugee agency COMAR, originally created to respond to Salvadorans taking refuge in Mexico, was directed to serve as a channel for United Nations help for this newly arriving population. The Roman Catholic Diocese of Chiapas also reached out to them, as did a variety of other international agencies.

Several of those who stayed in Guatemala were captured by the army, which now, firmly in control, apparently no longer thought it necessary to kill everyone. Paula Worby, a staff person with the United Nations High Commission for Refugees, recalled the army's inconsistent behavior at the time: "It will always be a mystery why, side by side, the army killed some people in some places and in others none at all. . . . It seems clear that they never thought they would kill everyone, just enough to send a message and cause the displacement which permitted for reorganization under the army's terms" (e-mail communication).

A few of the men who were captured were taken to the army base in Playa Grande and tortured for months. One described his experience in detail in testimony that was written into the play on the violence in Santa María. He was forced to drink urine and eat human excrement. Shocks were applied to various parts of his body, including his eyes, which left him with chronic eye problems. After months of this torture, the men were allowed to rejoin their families and move back to Santa María. The memories, of course, continued to terrify (Shea 1996).

Other families were not captured but were exhausted in the struggle to survive like animals. Then, in March 1982, they heard on the radio that a new president, General Efraín Rios Montt, had taken power in a coup d'état and issued an "amnesty" allowing those in hiding to come out without fear. They were being invited to come out of hiding. In fact, families that responded to his invitation were not harmed. Rios Montt's amnesty, however, did not spring from concern for the well-being of the campesinos. His move, rather, was part of a plan of pacification and control. And, although some of those who felt protected by his amnesty continued to hold him in esteem, Rios Montt's soldiers continued to ravage the countryside, killing thousands.

Some Santa María people who stayed in the country were relocated near the military base for a year or so, before being allowed to go back to the village in 1983. Others were relocated to a village near the Mexican border, called Ingenieros. When the original inhabitants were allowed back to Santa María, they were required to build their small houses in very close proximity to each other, so they could be better controlled by the army. At first the army set up a post of sixty to seventy soldiers. But after a time, the post was removed and the military checked in from time to time.

> One elderly man recalled his feelings as he entered the destroyed colony: "There was nothing, nothing. It was totally burned. It looked like an ashtray. To tell the truth, one could not hold back the tears." The old man stopped, reflected for a few minutes, and then added: "It took eleven years to build and just three days to destroy." He paused again and then in a positive tone said: "But here we are. We escaped death" (Manz 1988b, 80).

In a calculated effort to divide the community, the army had invited people in to farm the land left by those who were by then refugees in Mexico. The newcomers were of different ethnic groups from the original settlers, who were all K'iche' in language and custom. The newcomers were predominantly Q'ueqchi, though other ethnic groups were represented. Nearly all were fundamentalist Protestants, in contrast to the original settlers, who were Roman Catholic. The newcomers owed the opportunity to farm to the army and agreed to be loyal to it. As a result, the years until the refugees returned were characterized by profound division and mutual suspicion, a condition the army could and did exploit (Manz 1988b, 82).

As noted above, just two families joined the CPRs and, although the rest of the book will focus on the refugees and those who stayed in Santa María, the experience of one CPR family reveals a lot about the thousands who lived clandestinely for ten years. The first years were difficult, Emiliano Pérez said. When the violence occurred, his family experienced it directly. Two of his sons were shot and wounded by the army but fortunately recovered. Initially, the family hid in the forest with others from Santa María. But one by one the others left for Mexico. Pérez clung to the idea that his family should stay in Guatemala, but the number of ex-villagers with him was diminishing, and then Pérez and his family were alone—"Solito, solito, solito," he said (interview, July 1994).

After some time the Pérezes discovered people from other villages who also wanted to remain. The years 1983 and 1984 were very hard, but they found some food in the cornfields of people who had fled the area. But 1985 was even worse. They were constantly hunted by the army and had almost no food. They had, as before, to be constantly ready to move, sometimes after only three days in one place. In one afternoon, two of Perez's three children were kidnapped by the army. The family grieved, thinking they were probably dead. However, in a rare story of survival in the annals of Guatemala's "disappeared," it later came to light that the army had given the children to other Guatemalans. The son was found in 1993 living as a house servant in Antigua; the daughter, in December 1995, also working as a domestic. Sadly for Emiliano and his wife, neither child wanted to return to live with them. Two more children were born during the family's years in the forest.

These brief descriptions provide only the barest details about the suffering and horror experienced by the people in the path of the army's scorched-earth campaign. We can imagine some of the rest and marvel at their will to survive. As will become clear, they possessed a will not only to survive but to create a peaceful Guatemala based on social justice.

CHAPTER TWO

Reweaving the Pieces
Culture of Fear/Culture of Learning

*Almost all who stayed were fearful because we didn't want to die. . . .
So . . . the people who stayed were against organizing ourselves to
demand our human rights.*

—Man who stayed in Santa María

*[In Mexico,] we had freedom of expression, and we learned about
rights, rights in general, as well as about women's rights. . . . Back in
Guatemala, we would never have been able to gain that learning.*

—Woman who returned to Santa María from refuge in Mexico

IN JANUARY 1984, an Americas Watch report concluded
that "torture in Guatemala—whether performed by 'un-
knowns' or by soldiers and police in detention centers—is practiced
in pursuit of official governmental policy" (15). The title of that report, *Guatemala: A Nation of Prisoners*, names the reality the refugees
fled from as well as the reality that sharpened and embittered the
culture of fear faced by those who stayed behind. Guatemala had
become a prison, especially for the indigenous who made up the majority of the population.

Those who fled and those who stayed experienced life in dramatically different ways during their years of separation. Only by understanding the depths of these differences is it possible to explore the
challenges they faced in reweaving the altered patterns of their lives
when they came together again. Likewise, only by probing the extent
of the change in outlook of those who found their way to Mexico is
it possible to fathom the threat they posed to the dominance of the
Guatemalan army on their return.

Before examining the processes of cultural adaptation that occurred in Mexico and in Guatemala, it is important to note the features of the prison the country had become under its warden, the army. The refugees' knowledge of this authoritarian system, however vaguely they understood it, served as the backdrop against which they created their culture of learning in Mexico. For those who stayed, adapting to the authoritarian system was, of course, the stimulus for the culture of fear they developed.

Four features of the control system imposed by the military in rural areas enabled the army to develop an intimate knowledge of what took place throughout the entire rural population of the country. First, there were the largest geographical units in the control structure, the "development poles," of which there were six located in areas of greatest conflict. Development poles were organizing regions within which every aspect of life was analyzed for its control features.

Second, settlements were established within the poles, called "model villages," the Guatemalan version of what in Vietnam were called "strategic hamlets." Model villages were constructed under army supervision by forced labor to serve army control interests. Houses were crowded next to each other in violation of indigenous custom, making it impossible to manage small animals in the household or to grow fruit on one's own immediate land.

Third, the army controlled all the resources flowing in and out of villages, including all aspects of development, by means of the blandly named Interinstitutional Coordinating Committee (ICC). The ICC included, depending on the level of its structure, local people or regional representatives but always, in the early stages at least, a military person charged with managing the decision process. There was, thus, no way around the army regarding any aspect of improvement villagers might like to institute.

Fourth, and finally, by far the most insidious control mechanism was the forced involvement of rural men in civil self-defense patrols (PAC is the Spanish acronym), more commonly known as civil patrols. All men, from roughly the age of fifteen to sixty or older, were required to serve shifts of twenty-four hours every week or two, depending on the number of men in the village and the level of conflict in the area. When Americas Watch issued its report in early 1984, it said there were 700,000 men in the patrols. The army's official charge to the civil patrols was to protect the village from subversion, but their actual role was to serve as the army's agent in the pacification of the population. Service was said to be voluntary but was, in fact, obligatory, on pain of severe punishment. Open resistance sometimes meant imprisonment or death. In some towns civil patrols bought into the army system and became active military agents, using their authority to threaten and kill. In other villages the men suffered through their shifts, seeing no options. (All these control mechanisms are discussed in Manz 1988a, 37–46.)

Thus, people were not free to come or go. They could not express themselves without fear of retribution. There were open agents of the army and hidden "ears" (*orejas*) in every place, in every meeting. The entire rural area had become, in effect, a prison.

Outright use of state terrorism continued beyond the scorched-earth period, as the Americas Watch report makes clear:

> Scars are visible everywhere—the number of widows and orphans, the destroyed forests, burnt homes and fields, abandoned homes, the new gravesites in the cemeteries, the fear and the malnutrition. Some communities were abandoned completely for nearly a year. Not one community is what it used to be; a forced transformation has befallen each one. The terror does not simply stem from the cruelty of the armed forces or from the policies of a specific government—although both factors are obviously involved—but from the systematic application of force to maintain effective military control in remote areas of the countryside. As the social and economic realities of Guatemala have pushed many people to the brink of starvation, the army's tactics appear designed to demonstrate that there are even worse alternatives than hunger. The terror is sufficient to ensure that the population understands that no level of dissent, let alone rebellion, will be tolerated (59–60).

A year later, Americas Watch, in its next report on Guatemala, *Little Hope: Human Rights in Guatemala, January 1984 to January 1985*, indicated that the situation had not improved: "Torture, killings, and disappearances continue at an extraordinary rate, and millions of peasants remain under the strict scrutiny and control of the government through the use of civil patrols and 'model villages.' Guatemala remains, in short, a nation of prisoners" (1).

Little of any of this was known even in the urban areas of Guatemala, let alone in the rest of the world. Americas Watch reported that a newspaper publisher had told its investigators that "only five per cent of the repression in the countryside is being reported in all the newspapers combined" (1984 report, 40). Guatemala was being terrorized by its own military government and military—and the world did not know.

Clearly, the role of the United States in Guatemala contributed to the torture. Given its intelligence access to the Guatemalan military, U.S. officials knew what was happening. Yet, in December 1982, at the end of the worst year of carnage imaginable, President Reagan met with Guatemalan dictator/president General Ríos Montt in Honduras and declared the general had received a "bum rap" in all the human rights reports that had condemned Guatemala's savagery against its citizens (Americas Watch 1984, 135).

The next year, the Reagan administration moved to resume military and economic aid. Although that aid was aborted because of the murders of employees of U.S.-based agencies, the United States, during the early Reagan years, worked relentlessly to support the Guatemalan government in the repression of its people. Americas Watch concluded: "In light of its long record of apologies for the government of Guatemala, and its failure to repudiate publicly those apologies even at a moment of disenchantment, we believe that the Reagan Administration shares in the responsibility for the gross abuses of human rights practiced by the government of Guatemala (1984, 140).

Culture of Fear

Cultures, anthropologists tell us, constantly evolve as communities adapt to changing circumstances. The ancient Maya civilization in Guatemala survived the onslaught of the Spanish conquest, and the people managed to preserve central aspects of its culture through a history of violent repression. There is no way of evaluating which epoch was the harshest, but certainly the reconquest of Guatemala in the early 1980s was thorough in imposing savage control on even the remotest village. Those who stayed had to adapt to that particular brutality.

To be sure, those who stayed in Guatemala during the period of near-total army control also learned a great deal. Daily life in families went on in the context of the repression. Children learned their roles from teachers and parents. Adults learned to accommodate to the power of the military. In the cities some clandestine organizing went on that involved analysis and strategic planning, particularly as grass-roots organizations began to reform in the mid-1980s. But in the countryside, given the control system, the learning was more limited to figuring out how to cope in the face of very limited choices. The reality was that survivors lived in fear—constant, relentless fear.

Psychologists have studied what happens to people who must adapt to constant fear. Jacobo Timerman, reflecting on his experience in Chile, noted that psychoanalysts have concluded that harsh political repression is designed to cause psychological damage to vast sectors of the population. People subjected to terror experience "depression, anxiety, insomnia, nightmares, diminution of intellectual powers, difficulties in sexual functioning, changes in family and emotional relationships, apathy, loss of memory" (1987, 29–30). They lose the ability to distinguish between reality and fantasy. They experience a sense of individual impotence. "Reality becomes confusing and threatening" (32). People become, in short, the passive, malleable beings the army in Guatemala intended them to be.

As Elizabeth Lira, a Chilean psychologist who lived through the Pinochet dictatorship (1973–89) and worked with its victims, has noted, permanent political threat generates what she calls "chronic fear." Chronic fear is a "contradiction," in that the commonly understood concept of fear is that it is a response to a specific stimulus that is recognized as a threat. Constant political threat, then, generates "chronic fear that is itself an invisible violence that changes the very psychic structure of the person. When this is experienced by thousands of persons in a society," Lira argues, "daily life changes. There is the constant fear of pain, loss, even of loss of life itself." What we have then is a culture of fear (Lira and Castillo 1991, 7–8).

One evening a man from Santa María and I were sitting in the darkness on a bench at the side of his house. Speaking in a low voice, he described the difficulties faced by those who stayed in Guatemala:

> For me the experience was very different from that of our friends and relatives who came back from Mexico. What affected us who stayed here, more than anything, was a great deal of fear. That is what affected our people most, because they were very intimidated. Especially those who were tortured in the military base, where they were warned not to reveal what happened to them there. Also, we were told to avoid participating in organizations like those called "popular movements," which argued for human rights. That was totally prohibited. And for that reason almost all of us who stayed were fearful, because we didn't want to die. We wanted to live in this sacred earth that is so beautiful. There is no other life like this. So, because of this, the people who stayed were against organizing ourselves to demand our human rights (interview, November 1995).

This man knew that people who disobeyed had been threatened and in some cases murdered. Noting the role fear played in daily life, he said, "Because we are so afraid, we aren't motivated to organize and demand our rights, or denounce the abuses that have come from the authorities."

He went on to describe the threats, which were a constant part of their lives. One area that came quickly to mind was service in the civil patrols: "Any person who didn't fulfill his obligations, or who didn't want to take his turn, was charged with being with the guerrillas. Anyone who was against the civil patrols was accused of being part of the guerrillas. And this was what people were afraid of—they wanted to avoid having bad reports or bad treatment against themselves, so they felt obligated to do their service in the civil patrols."

Other threats, he said, came from the outsiders the army invited in to take over the lands of those who had fled to Mexico. These occupants, who were referred to as "newcomers" (*nuevos*), in contrast to the original settlers who stayed in Santa María, who were referred to as "old-timers" (*antiguos*). My informant said that during the whole time that the newcomers were in the community, roughly from 1984 to 1994, there was no peace. Hard-liners among the newcomers kept accusing the old-timers of being tied to the subversives.

My informant noted how the fear implanted during those years lingered after the refugees returned. Before the return, the army had emphasized to the old-timers that they were not to participate in any of the organizations of the returnees; if they got involved, they were told, what happened in 1982 would happen again. "That is what they say. If you involve yourself in things, you risk 1982 again." The man went on to say that the power of those threats had diminished but that a few villagers still were frightened of what could happen. At the same time, his ability to reflect on and describe the fear was clearly facilitated by the return of those who didn't experience it.

Another man who stayed in Santa María also spoke about the fear. "The army," he said, "had its way of working in the communities in the Ixcán area and had everyone under its orders. What the army said, what it wanted, we had to do." The civil patrol was a major source of the fear, given that the newcomers had come into the community at the invitation of the army and were willing to serve in the patrol without question.

This man spoke as well about the threats the villagers faced, particularly as he and other old-timers began to listen to the news and learn about human rights: "The newcomers said that human rights are of the guerrillas. If one accepts human rights, that person is with the guerrillas. And . . . such persons were not friends, were not members of the community. And they were reported to the military base. In that way the army maintained control also" (interview, November 1995).

This individual had a unique story regarding his decision not to participate in the civil patrol. Of all the men in the village during all the years of the patrol, he was the only one who made a principled decision to refuse to serve. Once he came to the conclusion that the patrol was violating human rights and draining time from work, he sought advice on what to do, turning to the local Catholic church for guidance.

When he decided not to take his "turns," the pressure came down on him, first from other men in the community. Then he was called before the base commander at the nearby Playa Grande military base, who demanded that he serve. Even in the presence of this powerful authority, he continued to refuse to participate, calling attention to the fact that he had served in the army and thereby fulfilled his obligation. He was also aware that the country's constitution said people could not be obligated to serve in organizations like the civil patrol.

The commander then sent orders to the "military commissioner," the army's agent in the village, to draw up an agreement with the community, to be signed by its members, that would give this rebellious individual three choices. He could agree to serve in the civil patrol or he could leave the community. If he insisted on staying, he would be killed.

The "agreement" was drawn up, but only eighteen men in the community were willing to sign it. The resister took satisfaction in this fact, but he decided to leave the community and lived away for the next two years (1992–94) until the refugees returned and the patrol was disbanded.

My conversation with this man was revealing. His story provided specific evidence of what happened when someone decided to go against the system. The men of the village would have been ordered to kill one of their own if he had refused to serve and stayed in the village.

The experiences of those who stayed in Santa María and in other militarized rural zones support Lira's finding that constant political threat leads to life-distorting chronic fear. Traumatized by the violence in February 1982, survivors in Santa María endured months of indescribable hardship living on the run from the marauding army. When they were captured or gave themselves up out of desperation, they were forcibly displaced, at best, or tortured, at worst. When they were permitted, after a year or more, to resettle in their communities, it was under conditions of absolute control and constant threat and harassment.

Contrasting Culture in Mexico

Those who fled to refuge in Mexico, including roughly half the population of Santa María, shared with those who stayed the terrifying experience of living on the run from the army in their cornfields and in the jungle. They were traumatized when they crossed the border.

By the time they arrived in Mexico, many had not eaten for days. One woman described how she and others crawled through sections of the jungle, with their babies tied under their stomachs to protect them from injury from the undergrowth. As they finally approached the border, her infant son was so dehydrated that he hung limply over her arm; recounting the story, she put a towel over her arm to illustrate the soft, lifeless form he had become. That baby, a young man at the time of the interview, stood beside her as she talked. They had survived the ordeal but just barely (interview, February 1995).

Another woman contrasted their lives when they arrived in Mexico with their lives in Guatemala:

> When we arrived at the border, we were a little more relaxed, because before we couldn't let the children shout. When we arrived in Mexico, it was more peaceful, and everyone could raise their voices, could speak. We were content, arriving in a place called Chajul, near the border. . . . Within a short time the Mexicans reached out to help us. They helped us a lot. But we were many, many people. So they didn't have the capacity to keep it up. Then, within a short time, came help from the church in San Cristobal, through the help of the bishop, Samuel Ruiz. We were more than five hundred families (interview, November 1995).

At first, the refugees were welcomed and given help. They mixed among the Mexican people. By 1983, however, the Mexican Commission for Help to Refugees, COMAR, had registered forty-six thousand of the Guatemalans in some ninety camps and they began the arduous work of remaking their lives. But the fear remained pervasive, in part because the Guatemalan army occasionally came over the border to attack the camps.[1]

Other circumstances also made the refugees' lives difficult. Their sheer number put a serious strain on the minimal services available and increasingly crowded the Mexicans living in the area. Further, COMAR was itself incorporated into the Mexican Department of the Interior and linked to the Department of Immigration, which had traditionally been involved with keeping undocumented Guatemalans out of Mexico. Finally, the refugees were not allowed to leave the camps without written permission, and outsiders were not allowed in (Conde 1983, 49–53).

A refugee from Santa María described that period: "I think those things happened more in Chiapas, because there *la Migra* [Immigration] controlled the situation. They said the refugees were subversives, and they had no confidence in us" (interview, June 1997).

The Guatemalan and Mexican governments both had compelling reasons for wanting the Guatemalan refugees out of Chiapas, which shares a long common border with what were the most conflictive areas in Guatemala. The Guatemalan military dictatorship did not like having a hostile portion of its population located so close to its border, knowing that the guerrillas moved freely back and forth. Likewise, the Mexican government did not want an organized, angry, foreign peasant population in Chiapas, its poorest state, where conditions were already volatile (Manz 1988a, 148).

So, after just two years in Chiapas, substantial numbers of the refugees, including nearly all those from Santa María, were forcibly relocated to formally established camps created for them in the Mexican states of Campeche and Quintana Roo. The process began in April 1984 and lasted for more than a year. Harsh measures were taken to make the refugees relocate: they were threatened with being repatriated to Guatemala; they had their food supplies cut off; and, in one case, a camp was burned to the ground, leaving them no base from which to struggle (Manz 1988a, 153). Most of the people from Santa María were taken to Campeche. About ten of the families that held out the longest were transported to Quintana Roo.

The Mexican authorities told the refugees that the move was for their own protection. The refugees speculated, however, that the Guatemalan government had put pressure on Mexico out of concern that they were helping the guerrillas from the Mexican side of the border. One of the returnees from Santa María pointed out that after the refugees were moved from Chiapas the guerrillas carried on at the same level, making it clear that the refugees hadn't been responsible for their activities (interview, June 1997).

When the refugees were finally relocated to Campeche and Quintana Roo, their basic needs were met but their movements were tightly controlled. Permission to leave for any reason often required

multiple visits to authorities for permits. The same Santa María returnee quoted above described the repressive conditions they faced
in Campeche:

> When we arrived in Campeche, it was like [it was before] because at
> first *la Migra* was in the center of the camp controlling things. They
> didn't let anyone leave to work, but because people had so many needs,
> they went out anyway, to work on neighboring farms. Young people
> left to work in the city. Sometimes the violators were punished, some-
> times fined. It was very ugly in those first years (interview, June 1997).

COMAR did offer training in a variety of practical skills, including carpentry, tailoring, and weaving. The agency also enabled the
refugees to start schools for the children in a way that was culturally
sensitive. The situation was different, however, with regard to health
services. Guatemalan health promoters and midwives were not allowed to use their skills; health services were permitted only through
COMAR-approved sources (Manz 1988a, 162).

The refugees' conditions changed for the better following an international conference (known as CIREFCA, for its Spanish acronym) held in Guatemala City in May 1989 on the refugees in the
Mexican–Central American region. In the spotlight of international
publicity, the seven countries that sent representatives—Mexico,
Belize, Guatemala, El Salvador, Honduras, Nicaragua, and Costa
Rica—pledged to "respect and promote fundamental principles of
protection for refugees, along with other principles concerning respect for rights inherent in the human person" guaranteed in international declarations of human rights. The participating countries
established follow-up mechanisms to ensure that the agreements
reached at the conference would be honored. The process proved to
be a watershed in the treatment of refugees in the region, including
the Guatemalans in Mexico (Garoz 1996, 12–13).

Despite the repressive conditions the Santa María refugees endured in Mexico before the CIREFCA conference, the returnees
interviewed for this book did not, for the most part, speak harshly
about the treatment they received from Mexican authorities, even
when invited to comment on it. Either the memories had faded or,
on balance, they felt their experiences in Mexico had prepared them

well for the return and it wasn't important to talk about the more oppressive conditions they were subject to in the earlier years in refuge.

While acknowledging that life in the camps was difficult, the
woman quoted above who described the refugees' experience on arrival added that "in one sense, the time there was a school for us. We
learned many things in Mexico." When I asked what they learned,
she said:

> We had freedom of expression, and we learned about rights, rights
> in general, as well as women's rights. So there were many things we
> received. . . . Back in Guatemala, we would never have been able to
> gain that learning. [Before the violence,] women couldn't participate,
> or perhaps we could participate but because our culture didn't support
> it, we ourselves devalued ourselves in our activities. By contrast, in
> Mexico we received help from the nongovernmental organizations, so
> we began to receive courses, many things (interview, November 1995).

Another woman returnee added her perspective on the orienta-
tion they received in Mexico and the reason the women organized
themselves:

> We organized to receive training regarding rights and how to manage
> projects so that we, as women, would have the incentive to participate.
> At that time many women were afraid, saying that only men had the
> right to participate in the community. But we women had the same
> right. So with that in mind, and knowing we would be returning to
> Guatemala, we organized ourselves (interview, June 1997).

As noted above, schooling was available for the children in Mexico. Most of the adults had not learned to read and write but had
come to realize how important education was for their children. So
they asked for and received help in preparing youth who had finished
all or a major part of their primary school education to become "education promoters"—teachers of the younger children.

One of these promoters described the satisfying journey through
which education became a major priority for the refugees. Shortly
after their arrival in Chiapas, he said, the exiles took stock and realized how many children had little or no education, because they had
had no teachers in the village for the four years prior to the scorched-
earth campaign. Once the new education promoters were selected,

the first step was to diagnose skill levels to sort the children into grade levels. The promoters then began to teach, very haltingly at first, then with more confidence, based on what they had been taught (interview, June 1997).

The villagers' training as education promoters took a more formal turn when they asked nuns from the church in Chiapas to guide them in the teaching process and give them some materials. After the move to Campeche, the education promoters took up the work of teaching again. At that point COMAR stepped in to help, offering not only materials but also the consultative help of a team of Guatemalan educators who had fled to Mexico as political exiles some time before the main exodus from Guatemala. The educators provided training in both teaching methods and content that emphasized the causes of the war as rooted in class oppression. They also helped the promoters think about what to teach the children about their Maya roots. This team worked with the promoters until 1988. By the time the team was withdrawn, the promoters had a high level of confidence and enthusiasm for their work.

At first COMAR was supportive of the focus on Guatemalan themes in the educational curriculum and did not interfere with the promoters' ideological desire to help the children deal with the causes of the war. That changed in 1989, however, when the agency informed the promoters that they would have to include lessons about Mexico, arguing that, having been born there, many of the children were Mexican. In fact, the Mexican ministry of education wanted the teaching to focus on Mexican content exclusively. But the promoters were willing to go only so far as to deal with the culture and history of both countries (interview, education promoter, June 1997).

The pace of learning among the adults in the refugee community quickened with the emerging sense that they would have to take the initiative if they were ever going to be able to return to Guatemala. Miguel Reyes, who was an elected representative to the refugee leadership group in Mexico called the Permanent Commissions, described this process:

> As we passed various years and nothing happened, [the tension rose again because] we wanted to return to Guatemala. So we began to

think again that if we don't do anything, we will find ourselves living [in Mexico] forever. We started then to negotiate. . . .We are speaking now of the period around 1987. Five years after arrival in Mexico, we began to organize ourselves in the Permanent Commissions in order to be able to start negotiations and dialogue in Guatemala (interview, November 1995).

Another man said that as part of their preparation to return they deepened their understanding of human rights. They realized, he said, that they had to be carefully organized. Among other things, they would need a good working knowledge of the laws of Guatemala and of internationally recognized human rights. Without that knowledge, they would be vulnerable.

On their arrival in Mexico, they had had only very vague notions about human rights. One man put it even more strongly: "When I left here [Santa María], I didn't know anything about human rights or the laws." Lacking that knowledge, they had been defenseless when their rights were violated.

The overall experience in Mexico was expansive, as this testimony makes clear:

In our refuge, through efforts of the church, UNHCR, and the Mexican COMAR, we received a lot of help and training regarding human rights: what are the rights, the laws that protect us, the constitution of our country that protects us, and the universal declaration of human rights that our government has committed itself to respect. So, from there, we refugees, the majority of us, gained an understanding of all of our rights—the rights we have as citizens, as Guatemalans. And we have this right to demand of our government that the government respect our rights and the decisions we take as a people. We have come to understand that Guatemala is a country that, as the government says, is democratic. And true democracy involves respecting what the people say and not what the government or the army says (interview, November 1995).

This knowledge clearly led to a great awakening. But up until that point the refugees had only information about rights and limited experience in the somewhat freer atmosphere of Mexico. The real test would come with the return to Guatemala and life under the control of the army.

Another vital dimension of the emerging culture of learning involved the specific steps the refugees took to organize for their return. To be sure, the refugees from Santa María and other villages arrived in Mexico with a base of organizing skills gained in working in agriculture cooperatives before the violence. They had put those skills to use and expanded them in recreating their communities in Chiapas and later in Campeche and Quintana Roo.

The refugees also developed skills through negotiating with the guerrilla organizations that had an active interest in when and how the refugees returned. The guerrillas' initial reaction was to put off the return until the refugees would fit the rebels' strategic interests. Events outran them, however, as the Guatemalans living in Mexico made up their minds to return with or without the guerrillas' support.

The Permanent Commissions found themselves squeezed on both sides. Their early sense of identification with the guerrilla cause led them to counsel the refugees against pressuring to return. But, after a tour of the camps in which the commissioners learned of the people's intense desire to return, the commissioners began advocating on their behalf, in opposition to the guerrillas. This dynamic honed the independence the refugees and their leaders maintained from the guerrillas, even as the refugees learned to think strategically in their interactions with members of the armed resistance (phone interview, Curt Wands, national director of NCOORD, November 1996).

One root of the organizing process for the return can be traced to a coordinating committee of the Permanent Commissions that was created while the refugees were in Chiapas. The work of the elected representatives to this committee was to facilitate the response to the needs of the refugees. After the move to Campeche and Quintana Roo, however, the three areas were sealed off from one another and travel was not permitted.

Miguel Reyes described the organizational process as he experienced it. The first step, he said, took place at one of the camps in Campeche. When President Vinicio Cerezo took office in 1986, the former residents of Santa María now living in Campeche sent him a letter asking for his help in enabling them to return to their land. They received no answer to their request. The following account does not include reference to the guerrillas, but a stream of activity between the guerrillas and Permanent Commissions was occurring in the background.

Details of the organizing of the Permanent Commissions in the camps throw some light on the struggle that went into the preparation for the return. Reyes described his experience as an elected representative of one of the two camps in Campeche. After January 31, 1987, COMAR facilitated a meeting with representatives from the other camp in Campeche. The next step was what became a yearly meeting with representatives from the camps in the neighboring state of Quintana Roo. Travel at that point to Chiapas was forbidden—though meetings were taking place in all three states.

When asked about his thoughts when he was first elected to represent his camp in Campeche, Reyes noted that initially the refugees had to secretly make connections with the refugees in Chiapas:

> The key is that we didn't think at all individually but tried from the beginning to form a coordination of Permanent Commissions from Campeche, Quintana Roo, and Chiapas. When we achieved the coming together of the three, then we formed the Permanent Commissions. From the beginning we had to do it without permission, clandestinely, particularly with Chiapas. When we finally were able to declare ourselves, the authorities gave us a place to mobilize ourselves. But before that, no (interview, November 1995).

Thus, this "space" to organize developed not because it was offered to the refugees but because they took it. Once organized, the Permanent Commissions began the process of preparing for the return. By this time a new attitude had taken hold. The refugees were still afraid as they anticipated what would happen to them when they returned to Guatemala. Reyes described it as a "tension of fear." But they also knew they would not be running in fear, as they had during the scorched-earth campaign. Rather, they would be returning with a mind to confront the situation. They now knew about the human rights ombudsman in Guatemala and about the national dialogue that had been going on in Guatemala City that was laying the initial groundwork for the returns and the peace process. Their information networks and confidence were increasing steadily.

In 1990, the refugees, represented by the Permanent Commissions, began to negotiate in earnest with the government of Guatemala, represented by its refugee agency, CEAR, in an effort to reach agreement on the conditions for the return. The historic accords, signed on October 8, 1992, were unique worldwide in that the government was bound to fulfill specific provisions between the refugee population and the government.

In brief, the accords provided that the return had to be collective and organized and voluntarily entered into, that returnees would have rights to free association and movement without restriction, that they could be accompanied by internationals, that security would be provided by all the rights in the constitution, and that they would have access to land, preferably the land they left but other land if their original land was not accessible or to new land if they never had it. Key subprovisions included the waiving of military service for the returnees for a period of three years and of ever having to serve in civil patrols.

Most of the specifics of the return accords were already provided for in the Guatemalan constitution, but, in the case of the accords, they were subject to international recognition and verification. The weakest provision, having to do with the refugees' access to land, was also the most important. The few refugees who had valid titles in hand and whose land was not occupied by someone else could take repossesion immediately. All others would be subject to various steps of mediation, negotiation, and legal action of indefinite duration—with an option to accept alternative land to be made available by the government. The bottom line, however, was that land would be made available to the returnees (a benefit that the internally displaced would not be offered) (Oficina Coordinadora, Conferencia Episcopal de Guatemala 1994, 15–33).

The process leading up to the first return was frustrating but also a time of learning and of experimenting with the use of various pressure tactics, including use of the international media. The process took from the October 8 signing of the accords to the following January 20, 1993, when the first group of refugees crossed the Mexican border into Guatemala.

At that point the government and the army still hadn't agreed on final permission for the return. But faced with delay after delay, some refugees decided to walk on their own to the gathering place for the return, putting pressure on the government to agree to allow the crossing. Some faced the prospect of five hundred-mile walks, a strong measure of their determination. Finally, permission was granted. One of the men who returned with the first group described the feelings: "We were already on the road. That was the victory, the gain in the struggle the people had organized. . . . On the road we got what we wanted. All the people were very much in agreement and very happy. When we were in Comitan [Mexico], and when the people heard that the government signed, then there was a sense of relief, of pride. Everyone was happy" (interview, November 1995).

One other agreement crowned the process of the return and gave the refugees great momentum as they crossed the border. Their goal was to make a grand tour through Guatemala's major cities, including the capital, on the way to their new community, which was close to the Mexican border. The government wanted them to take a short route that would get them to their destination without so much internal and international publicity. The same refugee described their goal:

> The government wanted the people to withdraw to Palenque, and from there to Benemerito, and from there to Victoria [the final destination], the short way. But we asked for the long way, because our idea was to denounce the government to national and international audiences, for the government to deal with things in the light, how it is that one government has its people in another country. And the government hadn't clarified that it had people in another country, in refuge in that other country. Our idea was to clarify publicly. . . .
> The truth was that that was a great work, an unforgettable history. . . . All the national and international people could see the entrance, the suffering of those who entered. The truth is that after that, when we passed from Huehuetenango, the people held us close to get the information—how was it, what happened with your leaving the country to go to Mexico. Why did you go to Mexico? Where did the idea come from to return? What is your idea in coming back again to Guatemala? They asked us all of that. And we gave them explanations. . . .
> Now the nationals and internationals knew, and we planted a kind of seed that we gave to everyone.

The combination of the two victories—the signing of the agreements on October 8, 1992, and the government's caving in, just before January 20, 1993, to the refugees' desire to return by the long route through the capital gave the returnees enormous momentum as they crossed the border. There they were greeted by Nobel Prize winner Rigoberta Menchú and a crowd of witnesses. In the following days, they passed victoriously through the country to great acclaim, climaxed by a huge rally and mass led by the archbishop at the cathedral in Guatemala City.

Those days were the culmination of the development of a culture of learning that had taken shape during the nearly twelve years the refugees were in Mexico, beginning with their experiential learning of what it was like to be free of the domination of the Guatemalan army. It had gathered force as the refugees recreated their communities in Chiapas and later in Campeche and Quintana Roo. They then moved on to more formal learning—how to be carpenters, teachers, negotiators, and so on. The climax of the formal learning was the workshops they received on human rights just before the return, during which the refugees developed an empowered sense of what it would mean to be citizens in their own country. That formal learning was complemented, finally, with the renewal that comes with successful organizing in the light of national and international media and pressure.

Challenges Facing the Returnees

The culture of learning the refugees had fashioned was profoundly different from the culture of fear experienced by the people who stayed in the country under the boot of the Guatemalan army. The experiences of the two groups, as well as the idea systems that shaped their thinking, created two dramatically different patterns. The question that drives this narrative is, How were the two groups able to reweave a reunited, shared pattern after the terror of 1982?

That clash of patterns would take place throughout Guatemala in the next years but particularly in the rural areas, where the army's scorched-earth savagery had driven people into refuge. But of course that dynamic took place in a context. Concurrent with the waves of returns that followed the first in January 1993 were a series of steps, halting at first, leading up to the signing of the "firm and lasting peace" in December 1996. That process took place in a still larger, international context—the globalization of the world economy, which has had a great impact on small countries like Guatemala. The new world economic order and its corporate leaders wanted stability and the end to civil wars, so private investment and "free markets" could have security in the pursuit of profit.

Given that larger context, the terms of the peace accords were contested, even after the signing of the declaration of peace. On the one side were the traditionally powerful, who wanted to maintain their privileges and benefits in the privatized global market. On the other side were the emerging grassroots groups, known in the Third World as "popular sectors," which struggled to strengthen the public sector. They worked to make sure all citizens, including the most marginalized in recent history, would benefit from a fair distribution of the nation's resources and opportunities. Only then, they argued, would there be anything like a firm and lasting peace.

Chapter 3 will frame that larger "contextual loom" in which the reweaving of the profoundly different subcultures of fear and learning took place. The peace accords will serve as the presenting framework. But the nature of the larger struggle will be defined by the relative strengths of the popular sectors and their powerful adversaries, represented by big business, its representatives in government, and a redefined army.

CHAPTER THREE

The Contextual Loom

The Peace Accords, Civil Society, and the Powerful

With some sectors of the country in virtual euphoria and others in cynical silence, the global peace accords between the government of Guatemala and the URNG were signed on December 29 in ceremonies celebrated in the National Palace in Guatemala City.

—Daniel Long, World Council of Churches
representative in Guatemala

THE EVENING OF Sunday, December 29, 1996, was typically cool in Guatemala City. In the plaza outside the National Palace, an estimated 30,000 to 40,000 people gathered to listen to proceedings marking the end of thirty-six long years of civil war that had left an estimated 150,000 people dead and a million uprooted. Giant television screens, set up to allow those outside to see the activities, functioned poorly, prompting some to shout, "The people are not represented" (O'Kane 1997, 1).

Inside the National Palace, four government representatives and four leaders of the revolutionary forces known as the URNG signed the Accord for a Firm and Lasting Peace, which formally ended the war. Guatemalan president Alvaro Arzú and U.N. secretary-general Boutros Boutros-Ghali signed the document as well. Some twelve hundred selected guests, representing forty nations, the United Nations, and the international press, were firsthand witnesses (Jeffrey 1997, 2).

People were relieved the war was over, but caution was in the air as well. An eyewitness described the scene: "The prevailing mood was of being at the ushering in of a new historic era. But the capital was not jumping for joy. The neighborhoods were calm, and expectations, it would later be said, were modest" (Hernandez Pico 1997, 14). The reality was that from the moment of their signing, the accords would be contested by opposing forces in the struggle to . define the identity of the country.

The ceremony featured the public reading of the Accord for a Firm and Lasting Peace by Foreign Minister Eduardo Stein Barillas. He said the accord represented a national consensus and proclaimed the country's concern for a range of themes that were part of the peace agreements: human rights, the safe return and resettlement of displaced peoples, truth about what happened during the war, respect for the identity and rights of indigenous peoples, and a participatory process of socioeconomic development. The signing of the accord marked the moment when all but one of the previous peace accords went into effect. The exception was the Accord on Human Rights, which became operative in March 1994, at the time it was signed (NISGUA 1997, 1).

The event at the National Palace was a watershed that brought previously clandestine forces into the open. When the URNG commanders had arrived the day before, they had been met at the airport by four thousand supporters—and, quite anomalously, by the army's official marimba band! Rigoberta Menchú, the country's Nobel laureate, was among those greeting the returning commanders. There were tears in her eyes as she welcomed them back to Guatemala (Jeffrey 1997, 2).

The night of December 28, the eve of the formal end of the war, thousands of URNG supporters held a public rally in the plaza outside the National Palace. An eyewitness described it as a scene of

> unprecedented—previously unimaginable—popular ceremonies
> and celebrations. At the plaza's acoustic bandstand, supporters of the
> country's guerrilla movement, the URNG, held a public rally. As if
> they themselves couldn't quite believe it, some of them still covered
> their faces with kerchiefs, the mark of the old clandestine mental-
> ity. . . . The lights of the majestic Metropolitan Cathedral gave off a
> surreal glow, while the buildings surrounding the Plaza were draped
> with banners (Jonas 1997, 6).

The next morning, the day of the official signing, many of the country's leaders led a massive march to the Guatemala City cemetery, where they commemorated the victims of the war. They took special note of the grave of Jacobo Arbenz, Guatemala's president in 1954, when the country's democratic government was overthrown with the help of the U.S. Central Intelligence Agency (Jeffrey 1997, 2).

These were moments when the popular sectors—the grassroots organizations of the people—felt a surge of energy. ("Popular" in this context means "of the people.") Revolutionary groups that had fought for the interests of the people were now there openly with them. The groups' supporters now dared to identify themselves, whereas only a short time before, allegiance to the URNG would have been denounced as treason.

Participants in these events might have been tempted to believe that the popular sectors were so in the ascendancy as to tip the balance of forces in favor of the impoverished majority of the population. That would have been an illusion, an understandable desire but not the reality. It was, nevertheless, a moment to celebrate.

As Jonas, a longtime Guatemala scholar and analyst of the country's social forces, has pointed out, the accords did not occur as a result of a triumph by either side and thus did not allow for the massive imposing of conditions by one side over the other:

> Taken one by one, the Accords are a mix of strong and weak agreements. They are certainly not the product of a revolutionary victory, but they do represent a truly negotiated settlement, much like El Salvador's of 1992. Brokered by the U.N., they have not been imposed by victors upon vanquished. Rather, they represent a splitting of differences between radically opposed forces, with major concessions from both sides. The obligations they impose on the Guatemalan government, including significant constitutional reforms, are written down in black and white; they are internationally binding and will be verified by the U.N. (1997, 6).

Jonas might have added that nowhere did the accords address the issue of land reform, the central issue for the majority, or the horrendously skewed distribution of resources in the society. Nor was she, at this point, calling attention to the powerful ties of Guatemala's elites with the global economy, which works against the interests of the poor. She was, rather, projecting the reality that both sides had given ground in the negotiations and that the way was now open for nonviolent, legitimate struggle. That, she argued fairly, was an important advance for all of Guatemala's people.

What would all this mean for the people of Santa María Tzejá and the other returnee communities and more generally for the people in rural Guatemala? Above all, for the people of the countryside, including the returned refugee communities, the signing of the Accord for a Firm and Lasting Peace meant the end of the armed conflict. People in Santa María, when asked six months after the signing what the accords meant to them, mentioned no longer hearing the bombing and no longer seeing army patrols pass through the village. The end of the fighting was tangible and a great relief. All else remained vague promises of hoped-for change.

A short time after the signing, one of the men from Santa María described a scene he witnessed in which a strange trio of actors appeared together. The three included Minister of Defense Julio Balconi; one of the guerrilla commanders, Rolando Morán; and Nobel laureate and indigenous leader Rigoberta Menchú. They had come to remote Cantabal, the municipal center of the area, which includes Santa María, to symbolize the newly harmonized relations of the peace process. The opposing commanders embraced and the speeches that day proclaimed that peace was at hand, but the bystanders had a deeper understanding. Noting the symbolism in that gathering, the man from Santa María said, "We know that peace will not be imposed from above. It is we who must make the peace" (phone conversation, May 1997).

The Peace Accords

Reflecting the deeply divided interests of the URNG and the government at the negotiating table, the final accords were strong or weak, acceptable or unacceptable, depending on the analyst's point of view. From the perspective of the popular sectors and their allies, three of the accords were generally seen to be strong enough to change substantially the balance of forces in the country if they were fully implemented. These included the Human Rights Accord, the Accord on the Identity and Rights of Indigenous Peoples, and the Accord on Strengthening of Civil Power and the Function of the Army in a

Democratic Society. (See Appendix 3 for the dates and places of the signing of the various accords.)

From the perspective of the popular sectors, two of the critical accords were weak. One was the Accord on Establishing a Commission for the Historical Clarification of Human Rights Violations and Violent Acts Causing Suffering in the Guatemalan Population—the hoped-for "Truth Commission." Its name revealed its weak nature: the word "truth" was not part of it. The other was the Accord on Socioeconomic Aspects and the Agrarian Situation, which avoided the fundamental questions of land reform and the profoundly unequal distribution of resources in the society.

The remaining broad agreement, the Accord for the Resettlement of Populations Uprooted by the Armed Conflict, received relatively little comment. Its strengths and limitations would come to light over a longer time period. Its one provision of interest provided for the creation of a technical commission that would assess the range of issues dealing with the uprooted populations and make recommendations.

The journey to the signing of the peace accords had been a ten-year process in Guatemala. In mid-1995, the URNG summarized its perspective on the history of the process to that point. The military, it said, had delivered the government to civilians in 1986, but the basic structure of the political system had remained unchanged. The country had not been demilitarized, repressive mechanisms were still in place, and there was no socioeconomic transformation (URNG 1995, 7–11).

The first tentative move toward breaking the deadlock on the long road to peace had taken place in October 1987, when representatives of the government met with representatives of the URNG in Madrid, Spain. The meeting was a one-time gesture on the part of the government in response to the accord signed by all five Central American presidents the previous August. But nothing came of the meeting (Jonas 1991, 165).

External pressures from the global community began to have an impact, however. David Loeb and Bernardo Alvarado summarize the several factors that even the army could not ignore:

> Both the United States and the emerging modernizing sectors of the Guatemalan economic elite wanted a stable environment for invest-

ment and trade that only a peace accord could guarantee. At the same time, with the collapse of the Soviet Union and the Sandinista electoral defeat in Nicaragua, the army command believed that the demise of the URNG was just a matter of time. As peace pacts ended the civil wars in Nicaragua (1990) and El Salvador (1992), Guatemala's generals decided they had little to lose by opening the door to negotiations, at least as a way to allow the URNG to surrender (1996, 4).

Two unexpected circumstances during the next period gave the popular sectors momentum to actively pursue peace. The first was the outcome of a March 1990 meeting in Oslo, Norway, when the government agreed to let the URNG meet with a variety of organized sectors of Guatemalan society. These groups included politicians, business leaders, religious leaders, and representatives of unions and other popular sectors. All but the business leaders saw the need for profound institutional changes. These meetings, which were lively yet serious, gave legitimacy to the hope that a peaceful resolution to the civil war was forthcoming. The government apparently hoped the groups would convince the URNG that it should surrender. If so, the gamble was a failure.

The other unexpected turn of events came when Guatemalan president Jorge Serrano (1991–93) attempted to take full state power for himself in what has been referred to as a "self-coup." Thwarted in his attempts to end the civil war, with the support of high-ranking army officers he announced he was ruling by decree. Congress and the courts were dismissed and the constitution was suspended.

In his brazen grab for power, Serrano misread not only the mood of the international community, which threatened to cut off trade, but also the popular sectors of Guatemala, which mobilized in force to demand that he resign. Disgraced, Serrano was forced to flee to Panama.

To the delight of the grassroots groups that had mobilized to oust Serrano, the Congress selected the highly respected human rights ombudsman Ramiro de León Carpio to finish out Serrano's term as president. De León Carpio took power, however, at the sufferance of the army and without a political party base of his own. In an effort to stabilize his role, he leaned toward army positions on issues and essentially froze the peace process. Again, as Loeb and Alvarado point out, the government miscalculated: "The lack of progress in the talks brought unprecedented pressure from the international community, and finally the government and the army were forced to accept what they had fiercely resisted for years: direct U.N. involvement" (1996, 5).

The role of international pressure is noteworthy here, calling attention once again to the larger global context within which the peace negotiations were taking place. Civil war was not good for business, and investors had stayed away. International corporate pressure forced the Guatemalan government and army to back away from its hard-line positions, thus providing indirect leverage to the URNG side of the table. If the war was to be brought to a close, the government would have to give on some points to get the guerrillas to put down their arms.[1]

In January 1994, the government and URNG signed an accord that gave an important place at the table to the international community, represented by the United Nations. Representatives of the United Nations would moderate the talks and verify compliance with agreements reached in the peace process. The accord also provided another role for the international community, by creating a "Group of Friends"—the six nations of Spain, Norway, Mexico, Colombia, Venezuela, and the United States—to ensure that the peace negotiations stayed on track (Loeb and Alvarado 1996, 5).

Of particular importance to the popular sectors, another provision in the accord created the Assembly of Civil Society (ASC). The ASC was charged with developing consensus documents on the themes, detailed in the next section, that would be addressed at the negotiating table.

Once these preliminary agreements were in place, the peace negotiations began in earnest. The Comprehensive Accord on Human Rights was reached in March 1994, with provision for its immediate implementation and verification by the U.N. Mission to Guatemala (MINUGUA). All other agreements would become operational only at the time of the signing of the overall Accord for a Firm and Lasting Peace, accompanied by the demobilization of the URNG. The next two accords were initialed in June 1994.

The first of these was the Accord for the Resettlement of Populations Uprooted by the Armed Conflict. The scope of this document was staggering; it mandated the resettlement of everyone displaced by the war. As noted above, the heart of the accord was the establishment of a technical commission to make recommendations at the time the final accords were signed. But the accord was weaker on the important access-to-land question than the one negotiated by the refugees themselves in October 1992 and would take the place of that one with the signing of the final peace agreement (Swedish 1996b, 14).

The other accord, addressing what happened during the war, was the disappointing "Truth Commission" accord. Those who lost loved ones in the violence had hoped for a more straightforward process that would name names and provide for the prosecution of those responsible for the atrocities. What they got instead was an entity that could say only whether a given crime had been committed by the army or by the guerrillas. Approval of this accord generated "howls of protest" (Jonas 1997, 8).

The next major breakthrough came with the signing of the Accord on the Identity and Rights of Indigenous Peoples in March 1995. Against a backdrop of centuries of virulent racism directed against its indigenous peoples, Guatemala will, once the necessary constitutional amendments are passed, be defined as a "multiethnic, pluricultural and multilingual nation." "If fully implemented," Jonas argues, "this agreement will require profound reforms in the country's educational, judicial, and political systems. It lays the formal basis for a new entitlement of Guatemala's indigenous majority, a right to make claims upon the state" (1997, 7).

That left two of the most contentious themes, the first having to do with economic issues, including land; the other, the key question of the army's role in a democratic society. With national elections scheduled for November 1995, peace negotiations were put on hold for the new government. Alvaro Arzú came to power accompanied by a majority favoring his conservative National Advancement Party (PAN) the following January. The new president moved pragmatically and skillfully to end the war, meeting secretly with the rebel commanders in Mexico prior to his election and firing several top hard-line army officers. Both actions helped set the climate for peace (Loeb and Alvarado 1996, 6).

Of particular note in the context of the people gaining voice, the 1995 elections also led to the formation of the Democratic Front for a New Guatemala (FDNG), the first leftist party to contest races in many years. Organized relatively late in the process, the new party showed surprising strength, electing six members to the eighty-member Congress, including three leaders of popular organizations. Also in that election, the URNG broke from its longstanding position of calling for the boycott of elections to urge people to go to the polls. Rebel sympathy lay with the FDNG, but the URNG was careful not to endorse the party, allowing it to maintain its separate identity. The election, however, marked a convergence of interests on the left and a new voice for the popular and revolutionary forces (Loeb and Alvarado 1996, 6).

The first fruit borne of President Arzú's commitment to end the war came with the Accord on Socioeconomic Aspects and the Agrarian Situation, reached in May 1996. The agreement was seen as a sellout by peasant organizations in particular and by all the popular sectors and by supporters of the URNG more generally because it failed to deal with land reform and the grossly unequal distribution of resources in the country. For that very reason, however, the powerful rich were enticed into the peace process as it moved toward its finale (Swedish, Feb. 1997, 8).

Next came the critical Accord on the Strengthening of Civil Power and the Functioning of the Army in a Democratic Society, signed in September 1996. Its most notable feature was a commitment to cut the size and budget of the army by one-third and to limit its role to defending the country's borders. A new national civilian police force would be created to deal with internal security. The accord also provided for major reform of the judicial and legislative branches of the government.

Remaining on the agenda was a final flurry of "operative" accords that were to lead to the final signing of the Accord for a Firm and Lasting Peace by the end of 1996. A major hitch occurred in October, however, when the government apprehended a leader of one of the guerrilla organizations for kidnapping an elderly businesswoman. Negotiations were suspended for a time and resumed only when the guerrilla commander of the URNG group allegedly involved in the kidnapping, the Organization of People under Arms (ORPA), relinquished his negotiating post to a subordinate. In the aftermath, the guerrilla leader apprehended for the crime was exchanged for the kidnapped woman. The incident further muddied the peace waters when it was revealed that a second kidnapper was involved who went by the alias of "Mincho." He disappeared and was presumed dead. In a bizarre turn of events, the government and the URNG denied Mincho's existence. The United Nations, accused at first of participating in the cover-up, issued a strong statement accusing the Presidential Military Guard (EMP) of disposing of Mincho. The kidnapping and ensuing Mincho affair weakened the legitimacy of all involved but was particularly damaging to the URNG (Hernández Pico 1997, 18).

Negotiations resumed in early December, leading to a definitive cease-fire accord, signed in Oslo, followed by one on "constitutional reforms and electoral structure," signed in Stockholm. The most controversial was the next accord, on "the basis to legally incorporate the URNG," signed in Madrid. Six days later, on December 18, the Guatemalan Congress passed a "National Reconciliation Law," based on the accord, to incorporate the rebel group into society. That law permitted the necessary legal reinsertion of the URNG by removing its liability for the political crime of seeking to overthrow the state.

But the law also incorporated a broad-scale amnesty for government agents, including military and police, who had committed common crimes in their campaigns to combat the guerrillas during the war. The law excluded from amnesty those guilty of torture, genocide, and forced disappearance, but it left a heavy burden on the victims to prove before notoriously weak courts that such crimes had been committed. Massacres and extralegal executions were not named in the list of crimes for which the perpetrators could seek amnesty. Passage of this law raised a storm of protest and legal challenges from human rights groups.

The one remaining accord, signed the morning of December 29, was the Timetable for the Implementation, Fulfillment, and Verification of the Peace Accords, which spelled out the dates for the demobilization of the guerrillas and the various phases of the process of implementation, which would last through the year 2000. That night, in the scene described at the beginning of this chapter, signatures were fixed to the Accord for a Firm and Lasting Peace, which initiated the implementation of all the accords (Hernández Pico 1997, 18).

These accords set the stage for a struggle to forge the patterns for an emerging postwar Guatemala. The popular sectors set out to make sure the accords would be fully implemented—not because there would then be a just peace but because fulfilling the agreements would move the struggle in a progressive direction and give it momentum. The powerful sectors, by contrast, resisted any aspects of the accords that crossed their interests, while signaling to the world that they were working in full compliance. That much was predictable, given the relative levels of power and access to resources at the time of the signing.

The Popular Sectors

Guatemala's popular organizations have a long and honorable history of struggle, including in times of horrendous repression. The heroic campaign of the Coca-Cola workers, beginning in 1975, which persevered through the murders of most of its leadership, is one notable example (Jonas 1991, 124).[2] Another powerful struggle was waged by the Campesino Unity Organization (CUC), which organized seventy-five thousand agricultural workers on the South Coast in February 1980, bringing the harvest to a halt and forcing the government to raise the minimum wage (Jonas 1991, 128–29). The list of such courageous struggles would fill an impressive honor roll. But the costs were frightfully high in repression, torture, disappearances, and murder.

When the first civilian president, Vinicio Cerezo, came to power in January 1986, there was hope of a new era for organizing in the popular sectors. The long years of military dictatorship had come to a formal end. A coalition of organizations, the United Action of Labor Unions and Popular Organizations (UASP), formed to contest the government on wages and working conditions. UASP included union federations, student groups, human rights organizations, and the peasant organization CUC. By March 1988, the alliance was able to negotiate an important pact with the government dealing with the control of prices, the raising of wages, and other issues (Jonas 1991, 181). But the commitments were never met. In May of that year, two army garrisons marched on the capital to challenge the government.

Only when Cerezo backed down on his commitments did the army go back to its barracks (Jonas 1991, 167).

As described in the previous section, the January 1994 accord between the government and the URNG called for the creation of the Assembly of Civil Society, which was given a specific mandate for the duration of the peace negotiations, after which it was to go out of existence. The ASC's main role was to discuss the themes scheduled for consideration by the negotiating parties and to submit proposals. With the signing of the final peace agreement, the legal status of the ASC ended.

Yet in June 1997, six months after its legal extinction, not only was the ASC still meeting but it had new life. Although it had started with ten sectors, the ASC had grown to include fifteen: human rights, religious, journalists, political parties, nongovernment organizations, research centers, peasants, Maya, the displaced, cultural groups, cooperatives, academics, women, elders, and a popular sector formed by students and workers (Sandra Moran, interview, August 1997).

According to Sandra Moran, a national leader of the women's movement, the sector groups knew they legally went out of existence at the time of the final signing of the peace accords. But in a critical decision for the development of civil society, they decided to continue and to take on the following major tasks:

> First, to monitor the implementation of the accords because we feel we are responsible for the agreements reached, and because it is the responsibility of the whole society to pressure the government to accomplish what it said it would do. . . . Second, to educate, so people know the accords, including their strengths and limitations. In order to disseminate this information, we need to organize. Third, to strengthen this multisectoral space so we can have a multisectoral vision of the future, rather than a sectoral vision (interview, June 1997; this interview is the basis for all of the following material on the women's sector).

These were huge tasks, especially considering that all the ASC participants were volunteers. But Moran was optimistic. Some of the sectors, she said, participated more actively than others: women, indigenous, displaced, campesino (peasant), and religious. As she continued, Moran described the work and organization of the women's sector, for which she was a key actor and an organizer of one of its groups, Nuestra Voz (Our Voice):

> Right now, we are in the stage of becoming a political subject, so we can negotiate with the government to make changes in policies—but to do it as a movement, not as separate small groups. We are trying to coordinate our actions. . . . Our vision is that we need to be together as one sector in civil society. And this is because all five of the major peace accords have sections on women's themes.

The women's sector had formed a national alliance, called Expresiones Organizadas de Mujeres de la Sociedad Civil (Organized Expressions of Women in Civil Society). It included representatives of five networks, five sectors, and fifteen departments (analogous to states in the United States). The sectors included students, workers, peasants, professionals, and cooperatives. The networks included people working on the problem of domestic violence and women's health issues, women in political parties, women who attended the World Women's Conference in Beijing, China, and the representatives to the women's sector of the ASC. The political departments were represented by their women's coordinators.

The Organized Expressions of Women represented women in what was called the National Forum, where the other party consisted of women appointed by the government to speak for it in negotiations regarding the implementing of the sections dealing with women in the peace accords. The accords, Moran noted, provided a framework for getting started, but the women's sector hoped to go beyond them: "Those accords are not only to be implemented. Just as important is the way they stimulate new organizations and lead to the mobilizing of people. That gives us the base of a new force to use in struggle and to deepen the accords. The accords are mechanisms to do that and to prepare for new struggles."

Another active social sector in the ASC was the alliance of indigenous organizations, which Moran said was further along in its organization than the women's sector. In a June 1997 talk, Juan León, founder of the Maya group Defensoría Maya and an organizer of COPMAGUA, the coalition of 150 Maya organizations organized in 1994 to participate in the ASC, spoke about the Maya role in

responding to the peace accords (presentation at conference on Guatemala, Washington, D.C., June 6, 1997; the material that follows on
the indigenous sector is from the same source).

This was the first time, León said, that the Maya population was
inserting itself in politics, based on its own experiences. This effort was a national project that involved creating unity in the country based on the society being multiethnic, pluricultural, and multilingual. It was a long-term project at local, regional, and national
levels. It would be based on dialogue with the population, with business leaders, and with members of some sectors of the army.

A major challenge would be to educate the population so that
everyone would know what the COPMAGUA project was. It would
involve, over the long run, recreating indigenous political systems,
involving how the people make decisions in their own communities.
Part of this process would be to recover a Maya legal system. For that
to happen, civil society, including indigenous peoples, had to develop an alternative economic system to the current one dominated
by CACIF, the chamber of big business in the country. Significantly,
the Accord on the Rights and Identity of Indigenous Peoples did not
address the economic rights of the Mayas.

Another critical task was to find ways to aid in the healing of
the indigenous population that was so wounded by the war. There
was so much disappointment, resentment, and hate festering in the
people. How to survive all of that? León noted that no one was dealing with the issues of mental health but that it was necessary.

The political challenge was to professionalize and activate the indigenous population so that by the year 2020 indigenous peoples will
have 30 percent of all the positions in government. On this issue of
time and its relation to the accords, León said that although the formal implementation of the accords was scheduled to be complete
by the year 2000, that would not be enough time. The issues in the
accords had developed over five hundred years, and they could not
be resolved in less than four years. León concluded, "We therefore
will not be bound by that timetable but rather continue to work until
the issues are fully laid to rest."

Yet another popular sector on the move in the ASC was the coalition of campesino groups, CNOC (National Coordination of Cam-

pesino Organizations). As Daniel Pasquel, one of its leaders, argued, land in Guatemala had been unjustly taken from its rightful owners. He detailed a history of the stealing of campesino lands by the big corporate agricultural interests. "We are saying," he argued,

> that we want to take back the land. We don't use the term "land reform," because then our enemies accuse us of being communists. So we talk about the democratization and use of the land. We are not talking about taking all the land for campesinos. Rather, we are looking for points of consensus with the government. We are proposing dialogue with the large landowners, but we won't accept the current situation where 3 percent of the owners have 85 percent of the land (presentation at conference on Guatemala, Washington, D.C., June 8, 1997; the rest of the material on the campesino sector is from the same source).

The core of the economy in Guatemala, Pasquel noted, was not gold or silver but land. For this reason, neither the government nor the big owners had an interest in complying with even the weak standards of the socioeconomic accord. So, he said, the campesinos needed to push past the limits of the accord to resolve the land problem. He called for international solidarity in the struggle for land, without which, he warned, there would be an uprising.

Indeed, there was an uprising in progress, involving two hundred land reclamations—or what the landlords call "land invasions"—on forty different plantations. The campesino population was desperate and willing to do what it had to do to get land. Half a million campesino families had no land and another million had such tiny areas that they couldn't support their families on them.

The women, the indigenous, and the campesino sectors were just three of the fifteen in the ASC. But they were among the most broadly based and active in creating new organizations and alliances to work for the implementation of the accords and beyond. The activities of these three sectors illustrate how the peace accords provided an important framework for their efforts but that they were not going to be limited by them. Rather, the accords served as a stimulus for organizing, which they hoped would carry the social justice process well past what was committed to in the December 1996 peace accords. These three sectors will be important to watch in the years ahead as indicators of how well popular movements are rising to challenge the continuing authoritarian tendencies of Guatemalan society. Moreover, all three have had a mandate to organize in rural areas of the country, including return communities like Santa María.

The Powerful

As the previous section illustrates, the popular movements were increasingly active in the period following the signing of the peace accords. They had energy and enthusiasm and engaged in a swirl of public activity. By contrast, the dominance of the powerful sectors was not new, and, for the most part, they called no particular attention to themselves. While the military was in the public eye in its determination to be seen as in compliance with "its" peace accord, as will be seen in Chapter 8, it worked tirelessly behind the scenes to protect and enhance as much of its traditional power as possible. As always, the national government, through the office of the presidency and key ministries, provided the leads for the media, but its deep agenda, oriented to the needs of the powerful, was not featured in its public image.

The rise of the Guatemalan military and its relation to the landed oligarchy was discussed in Chapter 1. Created to defend coffee interests, the army later expanded its scope to protect the owners of banana, sugar, cotton, and beef plantations. And land, as the description of the campesino struggle makes clear, was still at the epicenter of a latent (or actual, depending on one's point of view) social explosion in Guatemala. The structure of the country's repressive ruling system was tied directly to the control of land and the racism directed toward its original inhabitants:

> An important basis for the particular rigidity of Guatemala's class structure lies in having the most highly concentrated, totally unreformed land tenure system in Latin America. No less important as a key to the particularly violent and exclusionary behavior of the Guatemalan bourgeoisie is its centuries-long racism toward the majority Indian population, which has been essential for maintaining a coercive relation to the work force (Jonas 1991, 88).

Guatemala's modernization and modest industrialization were managed and controlled by the same families that owned the plantations. In that framework, the agro-export interests were not challenged by rising industrialists because the two sectors contained the same people. Rural power was, at once, urban power, and it was absolute in its rejection of any redistributive reforms. Furthermore, that power was reinforced by foreign investors, primarily U.S. corporations (Jonas 1991, 89).

An extensive infrastructure served the interests of the economic elites. The upper class was by no means monolithic in its interests and causes but came together around the key issues that defined the group as a class. Its central organ was a body known as CACIF—the National Coordinator of Agricultural, Commercial, Industrial, and Financial Associations. Founded in 1961, CACIF claimed to speak for business generally but actually represented the interests of big business. A range of think tanks and associations, many of which were supported by the U.S. Agency for International Development (USAID), provided support and back-up (Barry 1992, 147–60).

In addition to the business elite and the military, the other sector of the powerful was the political class, with the presidency at its apex. President Alvaro Arzú was elected in November 1995 and took office in January 1996. His successor will assume office in January 2001. A former leader in the sugar industry, Arzú had strong ties to CACIF and the business elite. His party, the National Advancement Party, Barry noted, "is commonly regarded as being the political project of the newly emerging financial and business elite." His central commitments were to that elite and to integrating the Guatemalan economy into the international global market (Barry 1995, 3).

By the time of the signing of the peace accords, the Guatemalan government found itself participating in a global economy in which the rules had changed. The Cold War was over. The "war" was now more purely economic: rich, developed countries against poor countries, economic elites against the poor within countries. Where before the Guatemalan army and government had been encouraged by powerful northern allies to fight communism, including violent suppression of armed insurgencies, now the call was to provide economic stability. Elites in smaller countries like Guatemala had come to understand that their role was to provide a platform for northern-based corporations to operate in an unhindered way, with a pliant labor force the corporations could hire at starvation-level wages.

In Guatemala, as elsewhere in the Third World, far from working as partners with the broad majority of its population, the government had become a junior partner—holding limited power—with global financial institutions, including the World Bank, the International Monetary Fund (IMF), and the World Trade Organization (WTO). These organizations, in turn, were controlled by representatives and the voting power of the highly developed, richest countries in the interests of their home-based corporations. The changed economic rules noted above stemmed from the rapidly increasing power of those transnational corporations that were able to demand and get open access to the economies of developing countries throughout the world. The name of the ideological flag they flew was "neoliberalism," rooted in nineteenth-century notions of unregulated "free trade," which gave a free hand to the powerful to exploit the weak—Great Britain in India, for example.[3]

Neoliberalism weakened the position of poor majorities in very specific ways. Its central tenet was the need to unleash the power of the private sector—by which was meant big corporations. This was to be done by cutting back the role of government to regulate on behalf of its citizens. Neoliberalism's doctrine devalued government—except in its roles in providing order and supporting the work of the private sector. It called for "structural adjustment programs" (SAPs) that undermined the position of government in what it could do for the poor. SAPs required cutbacks in health, education, and food subsidies; the removal of tariffs; the abolishing of restrictions on the importing of luxury goods and the ability of corporations to take all their profits out of the country; strict limits on wages and the role of unions; and so on. Corporations said they merely sought a level playing field; the effect, rather, was to clear the field of all barriers to the corporations' free exploitation of local resources and people. The poor were not simply marginalized, most were excluded.

Neoliberalism set countries against each other in cutthroat competition to sell exports needed to earn money to pay their foreign debts.

The World Bank and IMF, the leading institutions of neoliberalism, gained the upper hand in the aftermath of the debt crisis triggered when Mexico was unable to pay its foreign debt in 1982. Strict policies, including SAPs, evolved to deal with the myriad of debt issues in the Third World, as country after country was forced to turn its productive energy to paying its external creditors. Poor countries, dependent on one or a very few commodities for their exports, found themselves in a price war with other poor countries as prices plummeted while costs of imported goods soared.

These processes worked against the reweaving that was so vital to Guatemala's future. One analyst noted: "As the gap between rich and poor continues to widen, resentment and frustration build, tearing the country's social fabric" (Rosen 1995, 85).

The United Nations, through various of its agencies, had been calling attention to the dangers as well. At a U.N. conference at Midrand, South Africa, the onrush of economic globalization was declared to be irreversible, but its impact, if unrestrained by international regulation, would be the further marginalization of the poor. Dr. Boutros Boutros-Ghali, secretary-general of the United Nations, in setting the tone for the conference, emphasized that "the logic of competition needs to be replaced with the logic of solidarity" (Khor 1996, 4). To date, however, such cautionary statements are more in the nature of verbal tilting at gigantic doctrinal windmills.

Accordingly, the Arzú administration had moved aggressively to implement the neoliberal agenda:

> In spite of protests from labor unions, opposition political parties, and the church, the Arzú administration has hastened forward with plans to ban public sector strikes, evict campesinos from lands with contested ownership, and auction off a whole list of state enterprises—including telephone and electricity services, but also parts of the postal service and the highway system, and some services within the public schools (NISGUA 1997, 2).

In this, President Arzú was closely linked to the economic elite, represented by CACIF, with its central commitment to defend the private ownership of land as defined by its interests. Never ones to honor the sanctity of private property when peasants controlled or owned the land, the big landlords claimed absolute right when the land came under their control. Since coming to office, the Arzú administration had taken a hard line in favor of the landlords, using the police and the army to evict peasants occupying land they claimed had been unfairly denied them (NISGUA 1997, 7).

Meanwhile, with reference to the peace accords, the agricultural elite was angry with the government for not taking even stronger stands against peasants occupying land. Humberto Pretti, head of the powerful Chamber of Agriculture, claimed the peasants were using the cover of the peace accords to claim land that did not belong to them (Guatemala News and Information Bureau 1997a, 3.).

In the overall picture, the powerful sectors played from strength. For the most part, theirs was a behind-the-scenes force that carried forward from the previous culture of violence. And they had the money and access to the governing administration that would help them further their interests. For them, the peace accords were to be used, as much as possible, to give legitimacy to the traditional order.

Conclusion

With the signing of the peace accords, Guatemala entered a new, postwar era. Just what kind of era would depend on the relative strength of the opposing forces: the popular sectors with their international solidarity allies, on the one hand, and the powerful sectors with their international government and corporate allies, on the other. Advantage in terms of money, media, access to the bureaucratic resources of government, and the use of physical force all lay with the powerful sectors.

But the movement of the popular sectors and their allies to forge a broadly based project was under way. The role of the ASC as a multisectoral voice in the peace negotiations was unique to the Guatemalan process. Although little was expected of it from the powerful sectors that permitted its formation, the alliance produced an impressive series of consensus documents, most notably the one that became the basis for the Accord on the Identity and Rights of the Indigenous Peoples. But, more important for the future, the ASC became a platform for creating what Sandra Moran called "a multi-sectoral vision" for the country.

Initial efforts on the part of the three popular sectors described above were encouraging, particularly if they could unite through the ASC to select priority issues that all could support. As Daniel Pasquel, leader of the campesino sector, urged, agreement should be reached across sectors regarding priorities and then all should get behind them. "If we want to work for change in a particular moment, we need to move together," he argued (presentation, conference on Guatemala, Washington, D.C., June 1997).

Clearly, as well, there was overlap in the sectors. Women were at the same time indigenous and campesinas, for example, and so shared agendas across sectors. One of the segments of the women's movement consisted of representatives from sectors that included students, workers, campesinos, professionals, and cooperatives. Likewise, indigenous issues cut across all sectors. One key to success would be to maintain the ability to reach the level of cross-sector consensus that was pioneered during the peace negotiations.

Another key would be to broaden sectoral constituencies to include people in rural areas throughout the country. As Juan León cautioned, the challenge of managing the sectoral and cross-sectoral activities in the city, while at the same time finding the energy to train and send representatives to the hundreds of towns and villages in the countryside, was enormous. That would be the work in the years leading to the new millenium and beyond.

The issues and sectoral formations described in this chapter were constantly changing. By the time this book is in your hands, new problems will be at the forefront. But the relative strength of the powerful sectors will continue. The measure of change will be with the popular sectors, including their ability to unite around realistic goals and their power to attract international support for their efforts.

CHAPTER FOUR

Clash of Patterns

From Mexico and Guatemala

In May, we received the returnees. But within a short time, problems began to appear, because the two groups had lived so differently. . . . They made decisions in one way, and those who had stayed here decided things another way. Modes of relating and living were different.

—Man who stayed in Santa María

A T THE TIME of the first organized return of the Guatemalan refugees, in January 1993, the possibility of signing an accord for a "firm and lasting peace" was still an uncertain hope. As the refugees crossed the border, the only major breakthrough between the Guatemalan government and any segment of its citizens had been with the refugees themselves in the accords signed on October 8, 1992, which paved the way for the return. President Serrano's "self-coup" and the wave of mobilizing it activated were still four months in the future.

Yet the 1993 return ignited the population as the returning refugees worked their way from the border crossing at Mesilla along the Transamerica Highway to the capital. All along the road the returnees were welcomed as heralds of a new day for Guatemala. Their stories were eagerly sought out for the details of what the exiles had suffered and learned. Accurate information about the sojourn of the refugees in Mexico had been sparse within Guatemala. Official propaganda had tarred them as collaborators with the vilified guerrillas. Yet here they were in the flesh, with all the uneasy emotion anyone would feel on returning to a country from which they had fled in terror. They conveyed no sense of being hardened guerrillas but rather people like those who greeted them, who had also suffered horribly in the violence of the early 1980s.

70

With that, the atmosphere on the long path to peace changed. Refugees who had been cast as enemies of the state were soon resettled in a community called Victoria, 20th of January (for the date they crossed the border), under terms of the accord the state had signed with them. At a minimum, then, the currency of the government and army propaganda was devalued somewhat, which opened up additional political space. Managing the fallout from the triumphal return of the refugees, along with anticipating a long stream of additional returns, made governing more frustrating for President Serrano and therefore one of the factors that led to his failed grasp for absolute power.

The reality was that through the calculated ferocity of its scorched-earth campaign to crush the guerrillas in 1982–83, the government/army of Guatemala had created impossible dilemmas that would bedevil efforts to manage the return. Estimates place the number of those who fled to Mexico at one hundred thousand to two hundred thousand, which means that tens of thousands of farms were vacated by the exiles (Rader 1997, 31). In many cases, the "newcomers" who now occupied the refugees' land had been told the refugees were subversives who would not be coming back. With that assurance, the newcomers had settled in for the next decade and more, making the land and improvements their own. Under the best of circumstances, they would resist leaving. Meanwhile, the population in all areas had grown dramatically, adding further pressure to the highly charged land tenancy issue.

A major unintended consequence of the exile was the change in outlook and commitments, which made the refugees a different people as they prepared to return. The army had been able to drive them out but not to control what happened to them outside its territory. As Chapter 2 made clear, the two groups—the refugees and those who stayed—formed dramatically different perspectives and commitments while they were apart.

Taken as a whole, the refugee return process was enormously complex. Factors on both sides of the border added to the stresses and breaks in the pattern. The refugees' experience varied somewhat depending on the areas of Mexico where they lived; those in Campeche and Quintana Roo lived in more dense settlements and received better services, while those in Chiapas were more scattered and had fewer services. Guerrilla representatives moved among the refugee camps, seeking to influence the refugees' thinking and outlook regarding what was happening in Guatemala. As noted earlier, the United Nations, Mexican government agencies, and church and other nongovernmental agencies played major roles in training and consciousness raising among the refugees.

On the Guatemalan side of the border, the army saw the returning refugees as a threat to its control and worked to resist the returns in every way possible. Although it had been a reluctant party to the return accords in October 1992, once faced with the reality of return, the army worked to divide and demoralize. Its apparent goal was to divide the returnees from those who stayed and, where possible, to divide the returnees among themselves.

The perspectives offered in this chapter are enriched by the author's many trips to Santa María, beginning in December 1985. During the first several years, roughly half the population of the village consisted of original settlers, while the other half were people who had been invited in by the army to take over lands vacated by those who took refuge in Mexico. I was also in the village during the period immediately following the refugees' return, in May 1994, and for an extended period that July when the issues on the fault line between the returnees and those who stayed were most clearly in evidence. Several trips since then, through August 1997, have provided me with opportunities to monitor developing relationships between the two groups.

Those committed to helping Santa María through the Needham church's partnership with the village worked assiduously to maintain a balance with all segments of the community and supported only those projects that would contribute to the unity of the whole. The newcomers were our friends as much as the old-timers were, though the latter reached out to us more. During those years of our delegation visits, Santa María was deeply divided within. The stress and anger of the divide waxed and waned, depending on conditions, but they were ever-present.

Anticipation and Preparation for the Return

Three families in Santa María were in the group that crossed the border from Mexico on January 20, 1993, and marched triumphantly through Guatemala City and then north to Victoria, on the Mexican border, where they resettled. These three families visited Santa María often in the nearly year and a half before they returned to the village. Their goal was to work with the United Nations and other agencies to ensure the way would be clear for the refugees to come back. The men received a number of threats from the newcomers and were told to back off.

A dramatic moment took place in August 1993, when a U.N.-sponsored delegation came to Santa María to announce the refugees' return. The delegation included three original settlers from Santa María, two of whom were still living in Mexico. The third was Miguel Reyes, a member of the Permanent Commissions who was working in Guatemala City at the time on behalf of the returnees. He spoke at a meeting in Santa María, where all the men in the village and a few women—old-timers and newcomers alike—were in attendance. The atmosphere was highly charged. Reyes spoke in a dramatic, prophetic way to the hushed audience:

> We represent all the refugees of Santa María, and we are coming back. You who are occupying our lands will have to leave, and you should leave soon. We know that you, like us, are poor campesinos, and like us have a right to land in our country. But we have a prior claim to this land, having carved this community out of the jungle with our own efforts. We will work with you, if you like, to acquire other lands to which you can move—but you must leave here. We know that you have taken out loans on this land. We won't pay those debts, but, if you choose, we will work with you so the government will help you pay. We left here against our will, running like animals, but we return with pride and determination.[1]

The original settlers who had stayed in the community were overjoyed at that meeting, as their faces made clear. The newcomers, by contrast, sat in stunned silence. They had dreaded this moment, hoping it would never come.

On September 23 of that year, all the men from Santa María who were still living in Mexico came back for a one-day "extraordinary assembly" to work out the date and logistics of the return. The atmosphere was soured with the threat of a bomb going off at the assembly, but nothing came of it and the meeting took place as scheduled.

Plans were made for the return to take place early in 1994 (personal correspondence, Linda McRae, North American missionary with the United Church of Christ, who was at the meeting).

The newcomers, meanwhile, had entered into a process of negotiation to gain compensation for improvements they had made on the land and to secure promises of new land on which they could settle. When the offers seemed too low, they demanded an assessment of the improvements, which was done by a Guatemalan government agency. To the dismay of the newcomers, the majority of them would receive what they considered was still too little, based on the assessment. So they demanded that the assessment be put aside and went on to make truly outlandish claims. The government agency held them to the assessment; they had asked for it and they would have to live with it. Take it or leave it (conversation, Paula Worby, November 1995). By now, the newcomers were hooked into the negotiation process and agreed to leave on the terms of their assessments. Options were worked out whereby some could take higher compensation and no promise for other land, while others could take less compensation with the promise of getting help with land credits.

A major demand of the refugees, as a condition of their return, was the disbanding of the civil patrols. The government had agreed that the returnees would not have to serve on their return, so the decision of whether or not to continue the patrols concerned the original settlers who stayed: would they continue to patrol? The old-timers decided against patrolling, at least for a time (the issue of reviving the patrol would come up later), and the army came two weeks before the scheduled return of the refugees to decommision the patrol and collect the army-issued guns.

The newcomers left Santa María at the beginning of May, thus beginning the saga of the successful return of the refugees without conflict. Serious challenges still needed to be faced, but the date of the return was set and the process of reassimilation could begin.

What Happened to the Newcomers?

The fate of the newcomers was important because of its implications for other returns and resettlements. If, on the one hand, the newcomers fared well after they left, the news would spread that the government had followed through on its commitments with at least one group. If, on the other hand, they were abandoned to their own devices, that news would spread as well. Newcomers in other communities would stiffen their resistance to leaving on the basis of what had happened to the newcomers in Santa María.

Those newcomers who chose the higher payout with no promise of land credits were, of course, on their own in any case. A few did very well indeed. One man had owned the cardamom drier and received enough money to buy land in the nearby town of La Nueva Trinitaria. A Protestant pastor got credit for the chapel, his house, and other improvements, for which he received one of the highest payouts. Nine other families got land credits and bought some land on the banks of the nearby Chixoy River.[2]

But many others did not do as well. They were among those who had made fewer improvements to their land and for whom the money-only settlement was not advantageous. They were relocated temporarily to Cantabal, in an outlying section of town. At one time eighteen families lived there. They had been promised land credits but had received nothing. They had received enough money to support themselves for a time but not enough to buy land. Their dominant attitude seemed to be fatalistic. They despaired of getting help. Had they been able to organize, they could have put their case before the authorities. But they made no moves in that direction, probably because they represented three different ethnic/language groups and had little experience in working together. (This information was given to the author during visits to families in Cantabal.)

One by one, these families left on their own, most to return to their communities of origin. Their lack of organization meant they had no voice other than individual complaints. They were the new economically displaced.

The information about the newcomers results in a mixed story. Although some did well, there was nothing in their exodus to inspire other newcomers to leave their acquired lands voluntarily. It is reasonable to assume that word got out, and the history is clear that newcomers in nearby villages put up a stiff and effective resistance that blocked returns to "their" land. The fate of the newcomers after they left Santa María, then, has important implications for the re-settlement process more generally.

The Return to Santa María

Unlike the first returnees, who crossed the Guatemalan border on January 20, 1993, and made the triumphant journey through the countryside and capital before settling near the Mexican border at Victoria, subsequent Guatemalans returned with far less fanfare. In fact, those who returned to Santa María on May 13, 1994, came by air. They took off from Palenque in southern Mexico and landed at the only adequate landing strip available in the Ixcán, the runway at the Playa Grande military base. There they were greeted by repre-sentatives of the United Nations and other welcoming agencies. But soldiers from the base were all around as well, a violation of the agree-ment the returnees had reached for this return. Some people refused to get off the planes at first when they saw the soldiers.

During the months and weeks leading to the May return, the refu-gees shared and reinforced each other's determination to resist the army and enthusiasm to create a new society based in human rights and democracy. But that momentum and sense of community evapo-rated somewhat at the moment of return, first with the realization that the transition from refugee to returnee would be fleeting—an hour's flight at most—and that they would then find themselves standing on the homeland soil that they had fled from in terror those years before. Second, they realized they would be landing on the base of the same institutional army that had massacred their loved ones and burned their houses.

Once back in the village, however, the sixty-nine returnee fami-lies—some four hundred people (fifty-four families from Campeche, five from Quintana Roo, three from Victoria, two who had lived with CPRs, three who had lived during the exile period in Cantabal, and two who had spent the years since the violence in other com-munities in Guatemala)—found their stride as a people well orga-nized and energized to rebuild the lives that had been torn from them. An infrastructure was in place for them, including a newly completed road that made arrival in the community by vehicle possible for the first time ever. Agency representatives were on hand to welcome them and give them house-building supplies and food. All the attention in the first days after their arrival was showered on the returnees.

Those who stayed had dreamed for years of this moment, when they would be reunited with family members and friends. The return meant that the occupants who had taken over refugee land and divided the community were gone. This was to be a new dawn, a day of joy. There was a feeling of euphoria as the trucks with the returnees arrived from the army landing strip. One man described the anticipation of those who stayed:

> Before the people arrived—the returnees who are now in the community—those who were here very much looked forward to receiving them back, to live once again with them, because so much time had passed since these family members, these brothers and sisters, had left, and we wanted to be with them again. [While the refugees were gone,] we had had problems with the newcomers. . . . It may perhaps have been the cultures that clashed. We said that it wasn't like this before [the violence]. Better that these newcomers go somewhere else and we look forward to the return of those who had gone to Mexico (interview, June 1997).

But within days the euphoria of those who had stayed turned to a mixture of uncertainty and even resentment. The greater coherence of the returnees and their historic experience of planning and organizing for the return led them to act on their own and to seek out other returnees. Those who had waited so expectantly for them felt excluded. The same man quoted above recalled:

> In May 1994, we received the returnees. But within a short time, problems began to appear, because the two groups had lived so differently. It was difficult for one group to understand the other. They made decisions in one way, and those who had stayed here decided things another way. Modes of relating and living were different. They had adapted to the system in Mexico. Those who were here, well, we had to deal with a military system. . . . People here lived in the time of the civil patrols, when everything was militarized. We adapted to it and had to live like that. So, to make a rapid change at the time of the return wasn't possible; it took time to understand. I think that it

took perhaps a year for the two groups to understand each other once again.

Other factors were at work as well. The army had done its best to create a climate of suspicion regarding the returnees among those who stayed. The returnees, the army said, had associated with the guerrillas, were even aligned with the guerrillas, and therefore "bad" people. The returnees understood themselves very differently. They were not guerrillas and made immediate efforts to establish themselves as a hard-working civil population. But as a result of the propaganda, those who stayed had their guard up.

The view of a returnee was revealing in its contrast to the one who stayed:

> Those who stayed had a desire to develop, but they didn't have any idea of how to do it, of how they could work for it. "Why do you have so many ideas?" they said to us, "and how do you know how to solve your problems?" They went with all of their problems to the competent authorities, but at that time the competent authorities were at the military base. When we arrived, we didn't see things that way at all. We believed that the way to resolve problems was within the community . . . because to go to the base was to give information to the army (interview, June 1997).

Those who stayed felt dominated and resentful. The same man quoted above continued:

> Those who were in Mexico had certain opportunities to prepare themselves much better—women as well as men. During the time they were there, they put a lot of time into organizing and forming groups. . . . When the returnees came back, they imposed how things would be, saying, "We are smart. We are going to reorganize things here and introduce new methods." And the people who stayed didn't know how to do anything but to follow what they said. We had to adapt, but we felt dominated. . . . The fact is that there were certain leaders who came with them, who, according to what is said, acted very forcefully in Mexico, as well. . . . They were the only ones who could coordinate things. The problem arose from that.

In short, the returnee culture of learning ran headlong into the culture of fear internalized by those who had stayed. The underlying hope on the part of both groups, that they could somehow pick up where they had left off twelve years earlier, was dissipated. In its place was a standoff wariness and tension. Some could begin to bridge it more easily and quickly than others.

Another factor affecting both groups was the uprooting of some aspects of their indigenous Maya culture. Both groups had included a small number of ladino (the Guatemalan term for mestizo as well as indigenous people who have given up their traditional language and dress to "pass" as outsiders to the indigenous community) people, but the majority in both groups were indigenous Maya people who spoke only K'iche'. At the time of the violence, few women spoke Spanish and many of the men spoke only K'iche' as well. Ladinos in the village spoke only Spanish, however, so the need for language adaptation had existed all along.

The Maya heritage and consciousness have been topics of open discussion in several settings in Santa María since the refugees' return. They are part of the curriculum in the schools and were featured in a play written and acted by youth. But although various aspects of Maya culture continued to define the actions and attitudes of the people (e.g., use of the K'iche' language and the central role of corn in their lives), several returnees spoke of a lack of verbalized consciousness as they were growing up. One said, "I was never told anything specific about my Maya heritage as I was growing up. Nothing at all." Yet, because his family lived the Maya culture in its food, language, and dress, there was no particular need to talk about it.

With the violence and during the years of separation, however, Maya culture came under heavy pressure. One man who stayed added that certain traditions were forbidden outright, the use of firecrackers, for example. Other practices were discontinued because of fear. Militarization had a major impact on the culture. Within that framework, traditional forms of decision making within the community were undermined when everything that happened in the village was reported to the military through the civil patrol leaders and a military commissioner was appointed in each community. By the time of the return, those who stayed had internalized the army's ideology, which demonized the guerrillas and associated all references to human rights with subversive activity. Thought patterns regarding unity within the indigenous community, thus, were distorted.

The returnees had also had their Maya roots disturbed during their years of refuge. A key factor had been that different Maya ethnic/language groups had been cast together to live in close proximity in the camps. A progressive Presbyterian pastor noted: "It was in the refuge itself, when different ethnic groups came together. . . . They were mixing their cultures to form one collective. So they couldn't continue speaking their own languages, because the other wouldn't understand. So they needed Spanish. And clearly, the language doesn't come by itself but comes with the whole culture . . . which weakened [Maya] culture" (interview, November 1995).

The returnee quoted above about the tensions between the returnees and those who had stayed described his personal experience in this regard:

> In Mexico, we couldn't follow the values of our Maya heritage. We had to speak in Spanish, not in our own language. In my case, we have a son who is nine years old now who doesn't speak to us in K'iche'. He played with children who came from other language groups, so they had to learn Spanish to understand each other. . . . Now he is learning to speak K'iche'. In school they are learning the values and practices of the Maya. . . . Other countries have other customs. When we were in Mexico, we adopted customs that were not our own (interview, June 1997).

A woman returnee who is a leader in the united women's organization was playing a cassette of marimba music at the time of a June 1997 interview. She spoke about her love of the music but regretted that there were no marimbas in Santa María. She talked about the different dances her grandparents did to marimba music and how that music was very much attuned to nature. She would like to see a revival of Maya customs, she said; there were a few people, particularly older ones, who would like to revive the culture. But, she noted, the youth continue to slip away from it and wear traditional clothing less often, for example.

The Presbyterian pastor quoted above commented on his knowledge of the experience of the youth who were in Mexico. Some of them were affected by the more urban ambiance of Cancun. Many adolescents, he said, thought of themselves as pure Mexican. They rejected the mud and mosquitoes in Guatemala, which they knew only as small children. One could see the influence of their Mexican experience, he pointed out, in their way of speaking, dressing, cutting their hair, the disco music they listened to, and the way they danced.

The Mexican influence was particularly obvious in Santa María in May 1994, immediately after the refugees' return. Young returnees milled around the village center, dressed in shorts, the girls with modern hairdos and makeup, having no defined role and complaining of boredom. Based on what these youth had grown accustomed to, there was literally nothing for them to do. Some talked of returning to Mexico as soon as they could. Their dress and behavior contrasted markedly with that of the young people who stayed; the young women in this group continued to wear traditional dress, and most of these young women and men were married and beginning families (observations of the author, who was in the village at the time).

Three years after the return, one of the young returnees recalled the strangeness and tension they felt:

> When we first got back, I was very discouraged because when I looked around, everything had changed a lot. The land, as we say here, has a lot of hills and mud. By contrast, [in Mexico] there wasn't any mud, and we had good roads. . . . Many of us said that we didn't like it here, that we wanted to return to Mexico because of all the heat and mud that we weren't used to, and we had to use boots all the time just to walk, so we thought perhaps it would be better to go back to Mexico again (interview, June 1997).

This picture may be overstated. Indigenous Maya culture has shown a remarkable resilience through the centuries. The early 1980s was far from the first time that Maya culture was under serious attack. Language and dress are important dimensions of culture, but there is much more that binds a people. On this point, a longtime activist in Guatemalan issues, who lives and works with the Wampanoag people on Martha's Vineyard, Massachusetts, notes that although the language and traditional clothing of the Wampanoags have been lost, their cultural heritage is still strong (phone conversation, Jo-Ann Eccher, June 1997).

It is important to note here that Santa María was itself a "new" community, formed in the late 1960s to explore the possibility of colonizing the rainforest. The settlers took up residence in the Ixcán in the early 1970s. Community members had come from several different villages, though the vast majority were K'iche'-speaking Maya. The presence of nine nonindigenous families (ladinos) made this a mixed community from the beginning.

In a fascinating conversation in August 1996 about cultural issues, several women pointed out that they no longer held many of their festivals, played traditional music, or followed traditional medicinal practices when they relocated to Santa María. The older women remembered the customs and returned to their communities of origin on occasion for festivals, but they no longer practiced many traditional customs. There was interest, however, in reviving some of them.

The key point here is that both the returnees and those who stayed were separated even further from their traditional cultural practices by the violence and its aftermath. Neither group had been stimulated to strengthen, or even maintain, former levels of Maya consciousness. This left the villagers vulnerable, without the common base of cultural practices that would have helped fortify them for the challenge of reweaving the texture of their common community.

The two groups came together, then, with dramatically different visions for Guatemala, on the one hand, but with a weakened cultural core, on the other. The returnees were committed to human rights and democracy in a Guatemala where the army would be reduced to the role of defending the country's borders. Those who stayed had had little space to think in such grand terms. Their vision of security was based on accommodating to a powerful army, of being left alone to work the land and tend to family. But both visions were distorted as positions from which to come together because the cultural patterns they had shared at the time of the violence had been undermined on both sides of the border.

Fragile Threads across the Fault Line: The First Period

The fault line image will serve here to highlight the unstable, shifting, potentially volatile factors that had to be negotiated as the two groups rewove the fabric of their lives. The process of reintegration was very complex. Family ties were quickly reestablished, though with inevitable strains. Some people were more open and trusting and bolder in reaching out to former friends, now partial strangers. Tentative threads quickly reached across the faults in the fabric.

But the inescapable fact was that, as a result of their profoundly contrasting experiences, the two groups had developed very different cultural patterns. Issue after issue played out over the tear line between the two groups. In the weeks after the return, one woman after another among those who had stayed expressed fear about women returnees. They would say, as in a Greek chorus, about Mama Maquin, an organization for women returnees, "We don't know those people; we don't know what they stand for." Threads of suspicion ran through the whole group who stayed. They had been told by the army not to get involved with the organizations the returnees brought with them. The threat was that if they became involved, they would risk a return of the violence they had suffered in 1982. Besides, women who stayed had their own organization, El Progreso (Progress), which was safely not "political" and took up projects of benefit to the community (observations from a visit in July 1994).

Mama Maquin had been organized by refugee women in Mexico in 1990 as they found themselves stimulated to think about women's rights and how they could organize to achieve them. As a human rights organization, it did in fact pose a threat to the army's interests. And the army clearly had promoted its own line among those who stayed: don't get involved with returnee groups.

Among those who stayed, one of the most knowledgeable young men spoke about his anxiety over the stance taken by the returnees regarding the army. His position was that the returnees should find some accommodation with the army, some way of signaling they weren't openly hostile to the military. To his dismay, and he spoke for many others who stayed, the returnees seemed ready to bait the army, to defy it, to give it no quarter. That could spell doom for the whole community, he said (interview, July 1994).

Both sides clearly wanted to avoid a repeat of the terror of 1982. Those who stayed thought the way to do that was to accommodate, possibly by taking up some variant of the civil patrols, without arms. Returnees, by contrast, were convinced that the way to avoid a return to violence was to avoid the framework of dominance by the army as much as humanly possible. The accords governing their return clearly stated that they wouldn't have to serve in the civil patrols or their sons in the army for a period of three years. The returnees' strategy was not to provoke the army but not to give it any space in their lives either. An important part of their strategy was based in another of the agreements they had negotiated for the return—their right to an international presence. By having the regular presence of accompaniers in their midst, they felt that if the army tried to harass them, the accompanier would get the word out to international organizations and the army would have to back down (interview, July 1994).

So accompaniment itself was another issue on the fault line. A controversial fax received at the end of June 1994 from a trusted friend from Santa María illustrates this point. Its message to the Needham church was that the returnees didn't want any solidarity help in recruiting or coordinating the process of accompaniment in Santa María. That seemed strange because the returnees themselves had asked us to take just that role. But because of our trust in the source, we contacted the several people we had talked to about doing accompaniment and told them to hold off.

We found, as the matter sorted itself out, that the message had indeed been distorted, whether by design or mistake; we never tried to pin down. About twenty people who stayed had taken the position that they did not want us to support accompaniment. The fax clearly said, however, that it had been the returnees who didn't want our support. Those who stayed clearly saw accompaniment as a factor that would embolden the returnees to defy the army, which made those who stayed very nervous. Once the matter was clarified, the returnees went to great pains to make sure we did not respond to faxes or messages of any kind coming from people not authorized to deal with matters dealing with the return. We readily agreed.

For our part, we spent time with those who stayed, with whom we had seven years of trust-building experience, assuring them we were committed to the unity of the community. We reminded them, however, that our coming on a regular basis through the years had been a form of accompaniment, though we had never called it that.

Had we not been coming for years when there were very few outside visitors, we would have been identified primarily with the returnees.

That experience underscored the fragility of the lives of the two groups in Santa María. The distrust and resentment on both sides were deeply rooted. The potential was there for the community to stay divided or to disintegrate. Other issues were quick to surface.

One was the sharp difference in the way people talked about the guerrillas. Those who stayed tended to condemn, even demonize, them outright. Following the line of the army, those who stayed described the guerrillas as primarily responsible for the violence—at least in that they had so endangered the country that the army had no choice but to destroy villages to save them and the country from subversion. By contrast, the returnees had a more nuanced assessment of the guerrillas that included positive evaluations of their goals but also criticisms of their tactics. During their time in Mexico, some of the returnees had had direct contact with the guerrillas, so they were in a position to make a more informed judgment—and the returnees had not been subjected to the army's propaganda regarding the armed resistance.

Another difference was in the attitudes people took toward state-provided teachers and the noncertified education promoters—returnees with experience in teaching but who lacked Guatemalan preparation courses and degrees. In a community meeting with the regional school supervisor, he was asked whether he would authorize the education promoters to teach, as the returnees had requested. Those who stayed used the opportunity to argue that there should be more state-supported teachers. All the returnees argued in support of the education promoters, while only one among those who stayed was supportive. The upshot was that the promoters were allowed to teach but the state wouldn't pay them. The Needham church was able to help with that, making a commitment for a three-year period.[3]

In June of the next year, another teacher-related issue was on the line. One of the state-provided teachers had performed so badly and been drunk so much of the time that there was a movement to have him sacked. His colleague, the other state teacher in the village at the time, tried to defend him, using methods that were divisive in the community. He accused Randall Shea (known as Rolando there), the North American working with the schools in Santa María, of having charged the two state teachers with being agents for the army—and gave the names of four young men students as the sources for that information. He said, further, that there was so much danger and instability in the community that the civil patrols should be revived. The few who defended both teachers by minimizing their faults were people who had stayed. There was, however, a desire throughout the community to get the truth out. The incompetent teacher was, in fact, dismissed. The other state teacher did not come back the next year.[4]

Rolando commented that there was a tendency on the part of those who stayed not to accept that local people could be competent teachers. They had been conditioned to trust outside "authority" teachers who had degrees, even though ample experience had demonstrated the undependability and incompetence of the state-supplied teachers. This could be seen as one more way in which the people internalized their oppression by downplaying their own abilities.

As might be expected, as basic a cultural institution as the church also exhibited contrasting positions. Santa María had been organized by a priest, Padre Luis, who practiced liberation theology, based in the belief that God made a "preferential option for the poor" and that the struggle for social justice was very much the mission of the church. The army, in fact, had seen that theology and its practice as a prime threat to its control of the area. Priests and lay catechists were regular targets in the violent repression of the area. Those who fled to Mexico had been further nurtured in liberation theology. The organization they had formed with other refugees was called Guatemalan Christian Action (ACG is the Spanish acronym). Those who stayed, by contrast, had been allowed to express only conservative Catholic ideas, which largely avoided the social mission beyond simple charity.

In a revelation regarding the tensions, one of the catechists among those who stayed reported to the local priest that a Protestant group from Indiana had helped build a kitchen on the grounds of the Catholic church during March 1996 and that a Protestant (the author) had received communion. The priest was so upset, he threatened to keep Protestants out of the community. A returnee catechist reminded him that he had no power to do that. One upshot of the incident was that the man who brought the complaint suggested that perhaps there should be two Catholic churches in the community, one for the returnees and one for those who stayed. At that point, the priest back-pedaled, but the mere mention of that possibility revealed the deep faults that continued to run through the community (reported in a March 1996 phone call with the author).

Still another issue concerned the use of common land in the village. The rules of the community provided that some land would be kept in reserve as forest for the general health of the area. But that rule had not been enforced while the refugees were in Mexico. Some of those who stayed had grown crops in the reserve. On their return, the former refugees lined up support for the enforcement of the rule, giving violators a limited time to get off the common land. A few among those who stayed resisted this and the enforcement of similar rules, such as keeping animals out of the central area of the village. In an extreme act of resistance, one man suggested the possibility of a massacre on the scale of a recent one in Xamán, where eleven people had been killed and eighteen wounded, if the rule enforcement committee did not back off (interviews, November 1995).

The list could be extended, but the point is clear that on almost every aspect of community life the combined effects of twelve years of separation in sharply contrasting settings had opened up deep fissures in this once-united community. It is important here to see that even in a community that was seen as a model in its ability to come together, the challenge of reweaving was great. Noting these problems in Santa María provided a glimpse of how they would play out in other returns.

Emerging of New Patterns

In spite of all these problems, there is great reason for hope in Santa María. Noting the problems in sequence, as above, suggests each one was always evident with equal force. That was not the case. There was, in fact, a coming together over the three years following the return, and people of goodwill on both sides were working to heal the community. One man estimated that it took about a year for the two groups to resolve the most pressing and volatile of their differences. In fact, the reweaving continued for more than three years following the return, with the most notable differences continuing among the catechists.

One of the early hopeful developments was the uniting of the two women's groups to form the United Women of Santa María. That happened formally about five months after the return. A precipitating factor grew out of a proposal that the El Progreso group had submitted to get cattle for its members. A nongovernment organization had agreed to provide funds. When the women returnees in Mama Maquin asked to be included, they were at first refused but then told they would have to join El Progreso. At that point the Mama Maquin women went to the nongovernmental organization and told the group it was acting in a divisive way in Santa María and that if it continued, Mama Maquin would denounce it publicly. The nongovernmental organization decided to pull out of the cattle project, but the two groups decided to unite anyway.

Clearly, after coming together in that context, the issues were not all resolved, but at least the women were all talking together. The women of Mama Maquin continued to relate to the national network of that organization but did not meet openly in the community. One of the women from Mama Maquin confided that there were flag words the women didn't use in Santa María, such as "struggle" (*lucha*), a loaded term with a "subversive" connotation in the Guatemalan context. That the women chose not to use the word was an indication of their sensitivity and eagerness to knit the community together (interview, November 1995).

One man described the early coming together as two ears of corn that each had white and black kernels. Without having the racially loaded meanings those words would have in a U.S. context, he said the white kernels from each ear were coming together, as were the black kernels—his way of saying the progressives from each group were finding common cause, as were the ones he saw as negative in the unifying process. In his view, the hard-line negative folks were a relatively small group. On the other end of the spectrum were a few of those who stayed who were working closely in cooperation with the returnees (interview, November 1995).

Returnees describe again and again how they moved very cautiously to make sure the reweaving continued. In one case they wanted to form a health committee to manage the work of the health post. But when none of the people who stayed showed up, they put off forming the committee so it would not be seen as a separate action among the returnees.

By June 1997, the talk around town was much more about how the community was acting as a whole. A large grant secured by Padre Luis, who was now living in the capital, provided resources for the construction of several new buildings. Construction teams composed randomly of both returnees and those who stayed sweated together in the hot sun.

The one area of ongoing tension was within the church, where the lay catechists—who provide all the local leadership in the absence of a resident priest—still had ongoing differences about the role of the church. One of the catechists, a returnee, offered his view:

> In Mexico, we felt free to speak and had both strong internal leadership and effective resource people working with us. We learned to relate the faith to the constitution, to the laws, to human rights, and to think about challenging the military. But to those who stayed, that was wrong, equivalent to tying the faith to the guerrillas. But we are patient and won't try to force anything (interview, June 1997).

A catechist who stayed described life in the first two or three years after the old-timers were allowed to resettle the community. At that time the army was in total control of the village. Residents had to check with the army regarding any move they made. They were permitted to meet in the church for prayer, which they did two or three nights a week for mutual support. But, of course, he said, we were limited to a very "spiritual" approach to the faith—nothing to do with the social situation (interview, June 1997). That pattern, established in the early years, was internalized by the time of the return. Deep convictions about the nature of God are not quickly changed. But the catechists were meeting together on a weekly basis, discussing their differences.

So the tensions continued, but in a low-profile way. At the same time, new patterns were emerging. By far the most dramatic was the role of education in the village. Prior to the return, there were usually just two state-provided teachers, whose performance, as noted above, was erratic and who spent a great deal of time away from the village. Classes were offered through the sixth grade, but most students did not continue past the third.

By June 1997, the primary school had 216 students in seven grades, including a "preprimary" (kindergarten) group. And there were 113 in three grade levels at a junior high—which didn't exist prior to the return. All the teachers in the schools were education promoters and residents of the community, and many were learning to be teachers as they taught. The junior high school enrolled students from four other communities, making it a center of education for the region. In addition, there were six students on scholarships at the high school level in the capital city and three students in the university. It is extremely unusual for a rural indigenous community in Guatemala to be so involved in education (interview, Randall Shea, June 1997).

Within a year of the return, the state agreed to pay the salaries of the two education promoters who had the most years of teaching experience. Subsequently, a nongovernmental agency, PRODESSA (Santiago Development Project), became aware of the educational progress being made in Santa María and chose to make the community one of its education centers. Through its program, education promoters can complete the education necessary to earn state certification and thus be eligible to be paid by the state. PRODESSA understands education to be a political act and starts from the position that education should lead to the transformation of the community (interview, Guillermo Barrios, June 1997).

The education PRODESSA offers education promoters in Santa María and elsewhere is highly participative, involving its students (who are teachers in their own communities, including Santa María) in learning subjects from the perspective of their own reality. Students use methods the learners can then use with the children they will teach, with modifications appropriate for the ages of the children. The curriculum is progressive, drawing on current themes but also emphasizing Maya values. At every point students are stimulated to become critical thinkers by always questioning what they read and hear. One way this is done is by having the students write "parallel texts"—notebooks in which they reflect on what they are reading and discussing and develop their own critical perspectives (interview, PRODESSA team staff in Santa María, August 1997).

In August 1997, the author was able to observe the impressive work PRODESSA was doing in one of its educational seminars offered in the village. One session dealt with the theme of water sources and pollution. Another explored the global economy.

One important reason for the success of the schools has been the ongoing work of North American Randall Shea ("Rolando"), who worked as a teacher with the Santa María refugees when they were in Campeche, Mexico. In that period, Rolando was a long-term volunteer with the U.S. solidarity organization Witness for Peace. When the refugees returned to Santa María, he decided to make his home in the village and to continue working with the school. He was named director of the junior high school and was responsible for its reaching out to students from other communities. As of June 1997, eighteen teachers worked in the junior high, some of whom were advanced students in the ninth grade working with students in the seventh and eighth grades.

By June 1997, the schools in Santa María had taken a central place in the reweaving of the social fabric of the village. Earlier concerns among those who stayed that the quality of education might be reduced if there were no state teachers vanished. It had, in fact, become clear to all that the children who had received their education from the state teachers were the ones who had fallen behind. Young people spoke about how the experience in the junior high school had helped them overcome their initial uneasiness across the returnee/those-who-stayed line. After recalling how he and other returnee youth had wanted to return to Mexico when they found nothing but mud, heat, and boredom in their first days after the return, the young person quoted earlier emphasized that the dominant message three years later was that they had come to accept and like each other and could hardly remember what it was like at the time of the return. Two other young people heartily agreed.

The reweaving that resulted from enrolling students from surrounding communities in Santa María's school was equally impressive. The villages that border Santa María, including San José la Veinte, Santo Tomás, and Santa María Dolores, had all successfully resisted the reentry of refugees from those towns. The same was true of San Antonio Tzejá, some distance to the south of Santa María. When Rolando first approached the leaders of these towns, they refused to have their children enroll in Santa María because they didn't want anything to do with the returnees. But when they saw that Santa María was developing and their towns were not, they changed their minds (interview, June 1997).

A further educational development in the region was the introduction of education promoters in nearby communities. A promoter from Dolores was present at a meeting of education promoters in Santa María in August 1997. He had applied, and been accepted, to join a group of four Santa María promoters who were working over a six-year period for their state credentials during their vacations. Another Santa María promoter had worked for a brief time in another nearby community. So the idea of education promoters was taking root. To the extent it grew, it would lead to the displacement of state teachers sent in from the outside, who not only were often undependable but had little investment in the communities where they worked.

One scene that captured the regional changes took place in June 1997, when the fathers of students from Dolores and Santo Tomás built a kitchen structure in Santa María to be used to feed their children during the time they boarded in the village. Any animosity to having their children taught by returnees was gone. In the process, the propaganda that associated the returnees with the guerrillas dissipated as well. In its place was the social healing that came with working together on common projects.

As ties developed at a significant level, others followed. In June 1997, the author witnessed the championship round of a thirteen-week soccer tournament in Santa María that brought area teams to the village to compete. The evening of the championship match Santa María young people served a meal to 250 youth from the region. Although there had been soccer matches throughout the worst of the tense times in the area, a new spirit was evident. In fact, the junior high team from Santa María included young men from nearby villages who were enrolled in the village school. Thus, one level of outreach led to others in the deepening process of reweaving in the micro region of the Zona Reyna.

An important aspect of the role the schools played in the reweaving process was evident in the content of the curriculum. The pre-primary teacher spoke about doing some of his teaching in K'iche', providing a cultural bridge for students in the school. The fifth grade teacher described teaching Maya themes in social studies. In the junior high, the students studied controversial books about the area, including Ricardo Falla's *Massacres in the Jungle*, which describes the scorched-earth plunder of the Ixcán in 1982. Theater was part of the curriculum at that level, including dramas about the violence in Santa María at the time of the destruction of the village.

Students competed at the ninth grade level for scholarships to go to high school. Those likely to receive them were asked to sign a pledge that when they completed their studies they would return to the Ixcán region to begin their careers. This would not be legally enforceable, but it represented an effort on the part of the community to raise the consciousness of the students to an obligation to use their gifts to benefit and empower others who were living in similar circumstances (interview, Randall Shea, June 1997).

It is clear, then, that in the years following the refugees' return, new patterns emerged in the social fabric of this village, reaching to the several communities around it. Tensions remained, some of them still rooted in the villagers' contrasting experiences in Mexico and Guatemala. But the animosity surrounding those issues was largely gone. In its place was a palpable excitement about the schools and the potential of education to provide a better future for the village and the region.

Paula Worby, who worked for the United Nations, traveled all over Guatemala but had known the village for some years. She saw Santa María as a model of reconciliation:

Compared to so many other communities, Santa María is such a model. Whatever little quirks they are working out, they are still so far ahead of the game. Even though on a micro level you can see what is going wrong, on a macro level I don't even worry about Santa María. There is no way these problems are resolved in two or three or four months. It is basically a matter of time. In five or ten years, when all the kids have married, no one will remember who was born where. . . . The gut sense is that this is a community that is coming together, as opposed to communities that are coming apart (interview, November 1995, reinforced in conversation, June 1997).

Problems with Returns Elsewhere in the Zona Reyna

Santa María Tzejá is located in a subregion of the Ixcán known as the Zona Reyna. Like the rest of the Ixcán, it is a rainforest area that was settled as part of a safety-valve move to give land to peasants with too little or no land—in the place of more far-reaching land reform. The Guatemalan government supported settlement in the area through its land agency, the National Institute for Agrarian Transformation (INTA). The Roman Catholic church was involved in some of the organizing for the colonization process, including in Santa María. Today the Zona Reyna is made up of eight villages and several smaller communities and has some twelve thousand residents.

In a couple of cases, returns from Mexico have been far more problematic than the return to Santa María, and in other cases they have been impossible. Thus, although the relatively successful return to Santa María provided a basis for hope, the plight of refugees from other villages in the area who were returning, or hoped to return, dramatized the enormous task ahead for refugees, receiving communities, and internationals committed to supporting healing based on justice in Guatemala.

In 1994, refugees from the Zona Reyna villages of San Antonio Tzejá and San Juan Ixcán, both several hours to the south of Santa María on foot, negotiated the next steps of their return with the Guatemalan government. The San Antonio people faced organized resistance. Those opposed to this return and to other returns in the area had formed an organization, Regional Association of Landholders of the Ixcán (ARAP-KSI), made up of civil defense supporters from four different villages, including San Antonio Tzejá. In fact, leaders of ARAP-KSI were invited by INTA to an October 1994 meeting in Mexico with those who planned to return. ARAP-KSI's leader was

Raúl Martínez, a locally recognized civil patrol chief, with clear army backing, although actual ties to the army were not publicly known.

Agreements with the government were not honored, and the government land agency INTA manipulated land claims. As time passed, refugees from the two communities took matters into their own hands and marched back to their communities. Although the returnees to San Juan knew they could return to their community without conflict, they stayed with the San Antonio group as an act of solidarity. In June 1995, when the San Antonio returnees were barred from entry into their village, a group of five internationals accompanying them, including U.N. workers, was taken hostage for a twenty-four-hour period. The eventual outcome was that the returnees were allowed to settle on land that was part of the overall territory of the village but located a two-hour walk from the village center (Tovar-Siebentritt 1996; interview, Paula Worby, November 1995).

This story illustrates several factors operative in the region. First, the army took advantage of the natural resistance of the newcomers to encourage the formation of ARAP-KSI. Since the members of the association were civil patrol members, they came under the authority of the army, which could have told them to desist or even disband. Second, the fact that Raúl Martínez was still at large in mid-1997, with several warrants out for his arrest for crimes including kidnapping, spoke to the army's sponsorship of his leadership. Had the army decided to, it could have provided for his arrest, even though the matter was formally the duty of the understaffed police in the area. Third, the government's assurances to the returnees was worth nothing in the face of army resistance to the return. The result was impunity for Martínez and lawlessness in the region.

For the short run, at least, there was no possibility of reweaving between those living in San Antonio and the returnees, who formed a new community called Los Cimientos de la Nueva Esperanza (Foundations of New Hope). A wall of hostility and rejection was erected from the San Antonio side, with the army's evident support. So the new residents of Los Cimientos began to reach out to weave their lives together with those of residents in other smaller communities near them. That effort has been going well in the early stages and provides further evidence of the ingenuity and determination of the returnees (interview, Padre Beto Ghiglia, November 1995).

One segment of refugees from a community called Santa María Dolores (hereafter Dolores), immediately adjoining Santa María, decided to follow the San Antonio example and set out on its own to create a confrontation. The return of these refugees had likewise been delayed interminably by the government. Current residents of Dolores, however, made clear they would fight, if necessary, to block the return of former residents. Given the likelihood of a bloody confrontation, a mediating group met with the returnees and dissuaded them from their planned confrontation. Dolores refugees later agreed to accept the government's offer to find them other land.

Refugees from other communities in the Zona Reyna, including the villages of San Lucas, San José la Veinte, Santo Tomás, and Kaibil Balam, would like to return but find their ways blocked. Given the active role of ARAP-KSI in some of these communities, and the high level of resistance in all of them, there is little short-term hope that these refugees will be able to return. The greater likelihood is that they will have to accept other land and remake their lives anew. The Kaibil Balam returnees, in fact, have since been relocated to a new location in the department of Alta Verapaz (interview, Paula Worby, June 1997).

Conclusion

Ideally, Guatemala's refugees should have been able to return to the communities they left and peacefully reclaim the land they fled. As the Santa María Tzejá case makes clear, even when the returning refugees got their original land back, there were many issues to confront to reweave the life of the community. Santa María's experience highlights the fact that the refugees in Mexico and those who stayed in Guatemala had vastly contrasting experiences, to the extent that they shaped different cultures as they adapted to the conditions confronting them. The challenge of reweaving was difficult, but the Santa María villagers demonstrated it could be done.

An assessment of the factors the two groups faced in coming together in Santa María is important, because it brings to light the kinds of issues that surface under more ideal conditions. It therefore provides suggestions for anticipating and dealing with issues that underlie more complicated returns. Examples of the latter include situations in which those returning have to interact with people who stayed in the area but who were not part of the original settler community. That was the case in Xamán, where the return itself included differing language/cultural groups and the returnees moved onto land already occupied by people who had worked as employees on the land the returnees purchased to settle.

The experience of communities in the rest of the Zona Reyna makes it clear that the newcomers, with the support of the army, were successful in blocking the return of the refugees to their former lands. Except for the returns to Santa María and San Juan, the San Antonio Tzejá returnees were the only ones allowed to resettle in part of the overall territory of their village, and even here this area was considerably separate from the original community. ARAP-KSI, under the outlaw leadership of Raúl Martínez, had its way elsewhere, not only in keeping returnees out but also in a campaign to get land titles for newcomers.

Thus, conditions were set for continuing tension and fraying of the social fabric in the region. Army interests held sway in most of the area. Because of hostility to the returnees in the villages surrounding it, Santa María faced the threat of being isolated and vulnerable as a community that integrated returnees and those who stayed.

Given these conditions, the example of Santa María Tzejá in reaching out to offer students from surrounding communities places in its schools was particularly important. In these villages the newcomers had been victorious. Allowed to remain in their separated positions, with suspicions rooted in army propaganda, villagers bordering Santa María could have become increasingly hostile to their more successful but somewhat alien neighbors. But with the invitation to enroll their children in Santa María's schools, parents faced a briefly felt dilemma: expose their children to the tainted returnees (as they had been conditioned to view them) or enable them to continue with their education. They chose the latter, which led to such further integrating activities as the cooperation of education promoters from different communities and the building of the kitchen in Santa María. This and similar interaction extended the reweaving process from Santa María to the region.

These ties among several communities through Santa María's schools demonstrate vividly how the divisive power of propaganda is weakened when people are given real choices. The army script would have had the surrounding communities saying no to the invitation to enroll children in Santa María's junior high, particularly given that the curriculum included study of the massacres and participation in a play that enacted the history of the violence. But the parents said yes, and now the future leaders of their villages are learning to think and act in ways that may lead to more extensive reweaving of the social fabric of the region.

A Pictorial

LEFT ABOVE. The army guards a nation of prisoners. LEFT BELOW. Human remains from the violence of the scorched-earth campaign. ABOVE. Member of the civil patrol wearing an army T-shirt. *All photos by Derrill Bazzy.*

ABOVE. Easter morning in Chiapas. A Roman Catholic sister reads in the service. BELOW. Refugees crossing the Mexican-Guatemalan border. Some of the seventy buses can be seen in the mirror. *Photos by Derrill Bazzy.* RIGHT. Nobel laureate and Maya leader Rigoberta Menchú welcoming the refugees.

LEFT ABOVE. People in Santa María Tzejá who stayed after the violence of 1982, waiting to greet the returnees. *Photo by Randall Shea.* LEFT BELOW. Returnees unloading buses in Santa María. *Photo by Randall Shea.* ABOVE. "Long Live the Peace." Crowds celebrating the signing of the peace accord, December 29, 1996. *Photo by Jonathan Moller, © 1996.*

LEFT ABOVE. President Alvaro Arzú addresses the public as former guerrilla commanders, army generals, and other officials look on, following the signing of the Accord for a Firm and Lasting Peace, Guatemala City, December 29, 1996. *Photo by Jonathan Moller, © 1996.* LEFT BELOW. Corn-grinding mill, Santa María. *Photo by Derrill Bazzy.* ABOVE. Youth actors in the play *The Past Is with Us*, Santa María. *Photo by Randall Shea.*

CHAPTER FIVE

Resources for Reweaving
The Perils of Development

They say a lot, but in reality very little comes of it. As we say with regard to the economy, if policy was working, our products like cardamom, for example, would have gone up in price. But the price has stayed the same [low]. So exploitation continues, control of the few over the economy continues, and so we can never get ahead.

—Returnee to Santa María

T HE CLASH of patterns described in the previous chapter posed a challenge rooted in the widely varying experiences of the villagers who stayed in Guatemala and those who fled to Mexico. Together again, however, these two groups had to deal with the issue of how to respond to a flood of development resources. Both groups eagerly wanted to improve their quality of life, beginning with noticeable increases in their economic well-being. They didn't have to go far to find agents of development agencies with offers to help. Yet, as the comment above suggests, three years after the return and six months after the signing of the peace accords, the economic situation at the family level at least was not improving. That was true in spite of an array of development projects that were under way in the community.

There was, thus, an enormous contradiction for the people of Santa María and elsewhere between the outpouring of rhetoric and resources for what was called "development" and the reality—that their standard of living, already at a low level, was deteriorating. The government, meanwhile, was moving relentlessly in its project to graft Guatemala into the global economy, a process that featured the private sector of big-export agriculture and its related businesses. In that image-rich project of "free trade," delayed filter-down benefits for the poor, and reduced government, the peace accords fit uneasily. They needed to be complied with, formally at least, if the "peace benefit" was to flow as promised from wealthy donor countries.

Development was the watchword. But each sector wanted it in a way that furthered its own interests. For the powerful, and the government that represented them, the interest was in keeping wages down and maintaining a stable social environment, the conditions necessary to attract foreign investment. In that framework, the money that came in from wealthy donor countries could be used to respond to some of the needs of the population to convey the image that the Guatemalan government was doing what it could to help its people. The agents of the development process from that perspective were the development agencies, charged with implementing projects in local communities so that some basic needs, at least, could be met. At the margins were the residents of the villages and urban shanty-towns, the supposed beneficiaries of it all.

It was at the level of the people—the majority of the population—that the contradictions of development were most pressing. On the one hand, if "development" happened to them, without their deep involvement and decision making, they were mere objects of the action of others. On the other hand, if they were to take the initiative, define what they needed, and generate effective pressure for a living wage, for decent prices for their products, and eventually for structural change involving the redistribution of land and income, the effect would be revolutionary and the contradictions of development would finally be resolved.

The refugees returned to Guatemala against this backdrop of contradictions. The major returns took place from 1993 to 1996, the same period as the peace process, climaxing in the signing of the accords in December 1996. The government, on the one hand, used the returns as leverage to gain commitments for funding to enable the resettling of the refugees and aid them in their reintegrating with those who stayed. On the other hand, the return was potentially destabilizing, a threat to the country's role in the global economy.

In fact, from the perspective of 1993, the specter of upward of sixty thousand Guatemalan refugees returning from Mexico (the number represents the original forty-five thousand who were settled in camps, children born to them, and others who weren't in the camps) set off alarms in the halls of government in Guatemala City. Officials had a stability-threatening situation on their hands, resulting from the signing of the October 1992 refugee accords. The fear used to control populations in potential refugee-receiving areas would be harder to maintain in the spotlight of international scrutiny. Officials in both the civil and military branches of government knew the refugees had received extensive workshops in human rights and would resist military control in their return communities. The powerful knew as well that the guerrillas had been active among the refugees in Mexico.

Although the military couldn't predict just how volatile the return populations would be, the army knew it would need to engage a number of strategies to minimize the disruption. "Development" would be one of them. The military itself would participate in some aspects of this process, such as road building and repair, and would lead the way for the involvement of other powerful interests, including multinational oil and timber companies.

Thus, the stakes were high for all the parties involved. The government and military needed to work to maintain stability while, at the same time, seeking ways to exploit the resources of the area and benefit their allies. Other development interests, including a wide range of nongovernment agencies, were attracted to the region by the imminent return of the refugees. The people living in the area would be faced with pressure to get as much of the largesse as they could, knowing it could be shut off at any time. The returning refugees themselves were determined to use their organizing skill and energy to recreate the level of well-being they had known before the violence—and, if possible, to prosper at higher levels.

Profound questions about the nature of development course through the emerging history of the Ixcán. Development from the perspective of the human, democratic interests of the local residents was one thing. Development from the perspective of the nongovernmental agencies was another, with their short-term, must-spend-it budgets. And development from the perspective of the boardrooms of Texas-based Triton Oil and the big timber interests was another. Meanwhile, the rainforest environment was deteriorating.

Development from the People's Perspective

Padre Beto Ghiglia, a priest in the parish in Cantabal, the urban center of the Ixcán, described what, for him, were three distinct types of development. The first was people-centered, rooted in the identity, expressed needs, initiative, and full participation of the population, beginning at the most local levels. The second was the vision of development of nongovernmental agencies, which offered important services and projects but were not yet necessarily grounded in the vision and initiative of the people affected. The third type of development was defined by the actors and interests in the global economy, including their agents in Guatemala (interview, June 1997; subsequent quotations are also from that interview).

The first type of development, in Padre Beto's model, generated from the poor majority of the population. Advocates of that perspective on his list included the URNG as it was becoming a political party, some groups of returnees, and the CPRs. In his view, this was "a type of development that doesn't violate nature, that respects the rights of all the communities, that is available to everyone, and, above all, to the poorest and those most affected by the violence."

This type of development, he said, was the most difficult to promote with funding sources. From his perspective, to be done well, it would involve studies that enabled people to define themselves based on their own self-selected identities. In rural areas like the Ixcán, such studies would sort out the issues regarding the reintegration of returnees with those who stayed from the issues of demobilized guerrillas. They would identify the kind of development the people themselves dreamed about or desired. But, he noted, funding agencies weren't interested in starting with a careful investigation of what the people themselves desired. The agencies, rather, wanted to promote something that produced quicker results.

A flier for the nongovernmental agency Alianza (Alliance for Youth Community Development) describes development from a people-centered perspective as "a process in which a population becomes a 'social subject' through awareness gained from its own reality, where it takes its own destiny in hand and pursues actions that effectively lead to progress and collective well being."

The idea of the social subject was central to the thinking of Paulo Freire in his classic work *Pedagogy of the Oppressed*, in which he contrasted those who are self-conscious actors with those who are objects of someone else's action. Self-conscious actors—that is, social subjects—plan and take the initiative in shaping their own histories, or, he could have said, their own development, rather than letting it happen to them (1972, 21).

In Freire's well-known framework, people come to be social subjects as they identify and reject images of their oppressors that have been internalized. Lacking other models, oppressed people often appropriate an oppressor's way of life as their ideal, so that their unconscious desire is to be like the oppressor—that is, to become an oppressor of others. To become free, to become a social subject, is to reject that internalized oppression and join with others to work for common liberation. That struggle involves active learning rooted in the constant interplay of action and reflection. People trapped in oppression may initially need the help of an external agent/educator, but only in the sense that the outside educator helps the oppressed reflect on their reality in a way that leads to their own problem-solving initiatives, in which they see the solution as one they have identified (Freire 1972, chap. 1).

Development, then, from the people-centered perspective, must generate from the empowerment of local communities if it is to have integrity. Development cannot be done *to* people; rather, they must embrace and direct it. Freire and the Alianza approach are clear about this. Development, in its essential nature, is not about building infrastructure, or building anything at all. These activities are not ruled out as part of the process of building collective well-being, but they are not the heart of development. The essence of the process is people acting in their own behalf, reaching their self-defined objectives in a democratic way.

The second type of development, in Padre Beto's model, is offered by nongovernmental agencies and is more about building things and offering services. He described it this way: "[This is the] kind of development that works for the benefit of communities with short- and medium-term programs—not big projects like those possible for the oil companies, like providing electricity to the area. But they are projects like providing latrines, health services, potable water at a small scale, efficient stoves, and projects that benefit women. This is a type of intermediate development." This level of development, as Padre Beto saw it, provided services that were badly needed by communities. The underlying, and pivotal question, however, was how closely the agencies were engaged with the people's visions, plans, initiatives, and desire for full participation.

The third kind of development, in Padre Beto's model, was the one linked to the global economy. At the level of the Ixcán, this type of development was administered by the local government, with its center in the town of Cantabal. This type of development, Padre Beto said, was a very dynamic process and included promises to make electricity, potable water, and roads widely available throughout the Ixcán, a region that included 141 communities. But the allies of this process included international oil interests, represented in the Ixcán by the Triton Oil Company, and internationally linked hardwood companies. Further, this was the form of development supported by the army, which tied its interests with the globalization strategies of the national government.

It is important to qualify here that, although Padre Beto named the municipality in the Ixcán as linked to international big business and the global economy, that was not characteristic in Guatemala of municipal government as such. It was, rather, the nature of the particular municipality under discussion, where the mayor owned the local gas station and had ties to the oil companies. Key actors in the popular sector have, in fact, identified the municipal level of government as critical to their strategies and plans for democratizing Guatemalan government over the long haul. These actors want to see more power devolve to the local level, where the majority of people are likely to have better access to decision making and the resources allocated to local areas (interviews, Juan León and Rolando Lopez, June 1997).

In the Ixcán, the mayor's promises of electricity, potable water, and roads were attractive to residents of the area and, if delivered, would provide undeniable benefits. Decisions about the way these services would be made available, however, would be determined above and linked to external interests. For example, the army, for its part, saw itself as having a continuing role in road building, which served its project of maintaining some control of the area. And in this development framework, the environment stood to be seriously threatened by both the oil and timber companies.

It was clear, however, that people-centered development was not high on the lists of priorities of the big players in the global economy. As described in Chapter 3, the development challenge, as framed by the Arzú administration, was to insert the Guatemalan economy into the global economy as rapidly and as thoroughly as possible. That meant drastically reducing the role of the state in the economy, opening the way for private business and private investment. Privatizing government functions to the fullest extent possible was a cornerstone of the administration's program. In this privatized world, there was no place for rising wages or rising prices for the commodities the campesino population produced.[1]

Juan León, one of the leaders of people-centered development in Guatemala and the national coordinator of the leading Maya organization Defensoría Maya, shared his view about how the government practiced a form of development that contradicted the interests of the people:

> I believe that the government and the business elite that are running the government . . . are pressuring to change the laws . . . to make Guatemala into their private plantation, and now they are converting it into that. What they are really trying to do is to make private property sacred, rather than seeing the lives of people as what is sacred. . . . So for them nothing in life is more sacred than private property. And they want to make Guatemala—all, all of Guatemala—into private property. I believe that (interview, June 1997).

Thus, "development," is far from a neutral term. Its very definition, goals, and practices flow from the eye and interests of the beholder. For those particularly interested in development that generates from—and serves the interests of—the broad majority of the population, Padre Beto's model can serve as a good framework for analysis. Freire's treatment of internalized oppression as a distorting factor is useful as well, as are his proposals in the rest of his classic work for engaging the oppressed in a process through which they become social subjects.

An urgent question at the heart of people-centered development is whether the people themselves are fully in touch with their own best interests. This urgent question drives the rest of this chapter.

The Structure of Development in Guatemala: A Grassroots View

Pedro Chom, a health promoter and one of the leaders in Santa María, described the power structure of Guatemala as, from his perspective, it relates to development. His was a dramatic image with chickens as the players.

> [Guatemala is like] a two-story house of chickens. A few are above, and the many are below. Those above can stain those below with all the waste they generate. So that's the way it is for us currently, because the power is above. And we are under that power. By means of that power, based as it is in militarization, Guatemala doesn't have development. It doesn't have justice. And if there is no justice, there won't be peace. So this is what we came to understand, that this is our situation (interview, November 1995).

Chom's image was crystal clear. Given Guatemala's extreme polarization of wealth, the internal occupation of the army, and the grinding oppression, there could be no holistic development with integrity.

Yet, at the time he spoke, in November 1995, the Ixcán region was awash in a wave of what was everywhere referred to as development—the second type that Padre Beto described. Related activities were carried forward by "development agencies" with names and acronyms like CECI, Ceiba, Alianza, Asociatión AGUA, and PRODERE. These agencies were providing what the population agreed was desperately needed: roads, trucks, appropriate technology latrines, corn-grinding mills, school buildings, clinics, bridges, domestic animals, training in how to manage projects. Was this not development? Was there anything wrong with this picture, this process? Was this not providing just the kind of resources needed to reweave the fabric of life for the returnees and those who stayed?

Consider the possibility that the chickens in the upper tier of the coop provide the development resources—the roads, trucks, latrines, and so forth—for reasons that fit their own goals. Or that the upper-tier birds invite in peers from foreign coops to do the job for them. Or, alternately, they draw on army-dominated structures, like a re-named version of the civil patrols, to administer development re-sources (Popkin 1996, 35–38). That, Pedro Chom would argue, is not yet integral development. The birds on the upper floor give only of their excess, either to gain external approval and funding or possibly to head off a social explosion. Freire refers to this kind of aid as "false generosity" (1972, 26). What the agencies give, they can take away at any moment. As Noam Chomsky has observed, "Those who run the game can always call it off, turning ruthless at whim" (1996, 29).

Given the reality of the structure of the coop/world, there may seem to be little hope for people-centered development. The rich birds will never give way and will continue dropping on the poor as they see fit. Besides, the economic elites in Guatemala are aligned with the army and with the upper-tier birds in developed countries. In that framework, realists might argue, the poor had better grab whatever resources they can whenever, and as long as, they are avail-able and be satisfied.

Perils of Development: Experience of the Returnees

The returnees were not all alike, of course, or of one mind. Some adopted the realists' position that the basic structure wouldn't change so get what can be taken. Others, including the majority in Santa María, hoped to change the structure of the coop. Their vision was of a living arrangement all on one floor, where no group would have the power to drop its waste on another. The human rights courses they received in Mexico gave substance to their vision for a more just Guatemala, with more equitable distribution of resources. The re-turnee movement's successful organizing in achieving the accords of 1992 and the initial triumphal entry into the country all gave the returnees hope that they could turn Guatemala around. The challenge in the area of development lay in their determination to improve their lives, to seize every opportunity to move forward.

The critical question for this movement, however, was whether the momentum from the human rights insights and organizational success they had gained in Mexico would carry into the emotional dynamics and economics of development. Had the returnees become subjects—vision creators and initiators of their own development—in the sense Freire had of that term, or was there an essential piece missing? Did they have the internal cohesion and experience to deal with the distortions of externally devised development schemes to make development work for them, rather than having it, in some sense, happen to them?

It is precisely at this point in the process of consciousness that questions about the returning refugees have been raised. Clearly, the culture of learning they experienced in Mexico failed to offer an understanding of the pitfalls of development. In all the conversations I had with returnees in Santa María regarding the culture of learning in Mexico, none referred to courses or workshops on issues related to development. Everyone described learning about human rights and the training they received for various trades and skills. No one mentioned development. When asked about it specifically, two men in separate interviews said there was no anticipation of the issues of development. One of them remembered one workshop on quick-impact projects they would have available to them, but that was all. The other man remembered only that they were told they would have to work hard. No workshops had been offered in how to sort out development priorities or in how to plan for the development of their own communities (interviews, November 1995 and June 1997).

Now that the former refugees were back in Guatemala, the contrast between their treatment of human rights and development issues was striking. Leading individuals were named to serve as human rights promoters, to educate the community about this very important aspect of their lives. But there was no equivalent interest in naming "development promoters." No such term appears in their vocabulary. One agency, Habitat, trained people to be what could be called development promoters, but the role was not widely recognized in the community.

Several observers offered an explanation. The actual experience of refuge in Mexico, they said, especially for those who were relocated to the states of Campeche and Quintana Roo, was one of *receiving* "development" without having to ask for it. They had arrived with nothing and couldn't have survived without help. External agencies responded. The circumstances were unique to their being uprooted and resettled against their will in a strange country. Whatever the causes, the refugees became habitual receivers. And with all the training they received, little or none of it raised questions about the nature of integral development and the pitfalls of asking for external help as the first step in addressing all development problems.

Testimony regarding this outlook cut across the spectrum. Paula Worby, of UNHCR, noted that many of the projects undertaken for the refugees in Mexico, while heavily funded by the European Community, and sometimes successful, did not take into account the conditions refugees would face on their return. And "they didn't really have community participation as a variable, because it was this very artificial environment of refugee camps" (interview, November 1995).

Cristina Elich, with Habitat, focused on development education in the Ixcán. She described a project her agency was undertaking with refugees who were about to return, to help them anticipate problems they would face in the development process, because, she said, "if they arrive without it, it is already late." Her experience with returned refugees, and the contrast with those who stayed, is telling: "They come with the full security that everyone is awaiting their arrival to help them. So it is very hard to work with this group of people that is so accustomed to receive everything. . . . This group is very different from the people who stayed here. Many times the latter group show more disposition to work, and when they want something, they help themselves and do it" (interview, November 1995).

An accompanier who had lived and worked in the Ixcán Grande area for two years spoke of his despair over how people had come to look outside for solutions: "They have forgotten what they once knew—how to look to themselves for solutions. They won't generate the energy for independence" (interview, November 1995).

Padre Beto had similar observations regarding the returnees in general (though he noted that some returnees had adopted a more people-centered notion of development): "They returned with a very highly developed consciousness regarding their rights, regarding their position against the army, for example. But regarding their integral development, this is more or less a vacuum. We are saying their experience is on the other side, that they have had an experience of dependency rather than one of self-management. We see that as a limitation" (interview, November 1995).

Through no fault of their own, then, while they were in refuge the returnees had become accustomed to having their needs met, without a complementary consciousness regarding the implications for development of what was happening to them. They would have been perfectly capable of reflecting on that experience, as their eagerness to learn about human rights made clear. But, for the most part, they were not prepared through workshops or courses to anticipate or deal with the development issues they would face.

But although there was generally a lack of insight among the refugees regarding the need for autonomy in the area of development, circumstances varied from one camp to another and within subpopulations. The refugees in Chiapas, for example, were dispersed among more than one hundred camps and did not receive the intensity of outside help that went to the more concentrated camps in Campeche and Quintana Roo. As a result, the refugees in Chiapas became less dependent on receiving aid. Even among the camps in the other two states, there were differences in degrees regarding the dependence on outside resources.

The next two sections, on Santa María and the Ixcán Grande, describe two very different experiences regarding the issues of development. The most prominent difference was that in the case of Santa María, the refugee group returned to reweave its life with a group that had stayed in Guatemala. In the case of the Ixcán Grande, the entire group consisted of returnees.

Santa María

The majority of the refugees in Santa María had lived together in the Maya Tecun Camp in Campeche and so had common experiences. When they and the few families from Quintana Roo arrived back in the village in May 1994, they rejoined the original settlers who had stayed. So, although the community was divided along the fault line described in Chapter 4, the refugees were rejoining relatives and long-separated friends. This provided a somewhat more coherent base from which to think about development.

But even Santa María, remote as it was, was directly affected by the world economy. One saw backpack sprayers, used to spread toxic agents that killed weeds and pests. The village store sold containers of chemicals, many of them banned from use in the United States, with warnings in English—evidence of the impact of large trans-national corporations. But nothing captured the link these rural cam-pesinos had to the global economy more than the refrain that "there is no price for our products. Nothing we know how to do brings a price that will help us get ahead." People did not have specific knowl-edge about the global economy, but they were heavily affected by it (interviews, November 1995 and June 1997).

A lack of hard critical insight about development issues was evi-dent in Santa María as well. It was represented by the attitude that, whatever the need, the first step in the solution was to get external funding. Missing was a clearly articulated framework for controlling development, based on a coherent plan, for which resources were being sought and for which the community would struggle with or without external resources. It was just this kind of plan and com-mitment that would have positioned the community in the national struggle for social justice. Lacking it, the community was vulnerable to distortion and disillusionment.

It is important to add that some consciousness of the need to con-trol development as social subjects, as people in charge of the process, was evident in Santa María. But it hadn't evolved as a coherent whole. Given the fault lines in the community, that wasn't surprising. In as-sessing the community against a standard of holistic development, however, the question of how well the people controlled their own development is important to explore.

Pedro Canil, a community leader, described the expectations the refugees had regarding the aid they would receive when they returned to Guatemala. The people had been discussing the matter in Mexico:

Before we returned, we were commenting there that when we arrived here we would be receiving a great deal of help on the part of various agencies that would be giving money, especially the European Economic Community—which had designated various millions of dollars for the development of the Ixcán. Also, UNHCR, before we came here, had told us they would have programs, as they called them, of "rapid impact," in which there would be, for example, one head of cattle for each family. There would be twenty-five chickens for every family as well (interview, November 1995).

He went on to speak of his disillusionment, because the agencies hadn't followed through. The cattle and chickens were supposed to arrive within six months after the refugees returned, but a year and seven months later, they had not been delivered. (Half the promised chickens did arrive later.)

Canil described a number of community projects that had come through under the "quick-impact" category: a cardamom drier, corn-grinding mills, bridges, a truck, and stoves and latrines. He spoke appreciatively as well of the projects the Needham church had engaged in with the community, including building a basketball court for the youth and providing training for health services promoters and salaries for unlicensed education promoters who were now teaching in the community.

But all the items on Canil's list of unfulfilled promises and completed projects had one thing in common: their dependence on external funding. This very thoughtful man approached each development need from the perspective of whether the village could receive external aid. Another time he said, "It hurts us to have to ask for money, but we have nothing. And if we are working so hard, how can donors imagine we are becoming dependent?"

Miguel Reyes, perhaps the most dynamic of Santa María's leaders, looked at the development question somewhat differently. He was acutely aware of the need to avoid dependence on outside debt. The key for him was that whatever money was coming to the community should come as a donation, leaving no accumulated debt. "If we took the money from a bank," he said, "they could call in the debt and we would lose the parcels [farmland]" (interview, November 1995). But, although he wanted to avoid debt dependence, Miguel was far from averse to seeking outside funding. In fact, he was one of the point people in seeking it.

In July 1994, Miguel returned from a lengthy trip to Guatemala

City, where he had been seeking funding for Santa María. He noted in a meeting of the whole community that as a member of the Permanent Commissions he had become aware of how the United Nations was trying to get money for the returned refugees. "We need to get that money," he said, "not just for the returned but for everyone." (The author was at the meeting at which Reyes made this comment.)

Reyes then painted a powerful vision for the community, in which he talked about the streets in the Santa María of the future. At that point, only muddy footpaths connected the one inadequate road to the community. And the road itself had been completed in the context of the refugees' return. The streets he imagined would be more than thirty feet wide, so cars could use them.

Expanding further, he asked, "Who is the future?" People responded, "Our grandchildren." He noted that the adults would be in the cemetery by the time their grandchildren were in charge. He pushed people to think how big the population would be and where married couples would live.

Another theme he developed was the need to reforest. He made a specific proposal, starting with a thousand trees. Still another theme was the need for dignified housing.

All of these projects would take money, and Reyes had been active in seeking it with foundations and international agencies. His perspective, clearly, was to avoid debt dependence. His bold vision was calculated to energize people to plan and act together to build the future.

The lingering question was whether Reyes had the underlying insight about integral development, about the need to unite the whole community in an approach to development, that would draw first and foremost on the community's internal coherence and resources. To all appearances, he had good insight in that regard, as evidenced by the fact that he asked people to meet by geographical sectors of the community to determine where the streets would be located in their part of the village. But there was weak follow-through on that initiative, and the community as a whole did not generate an overall plan.

The potential of external resources to undermine a community was expressed most eloquently by Padre Luis Gurriarán, the priest who originally organized Santa María and who had to flee for his life in the fall of 1976. He was back in the community in June 1995, offering a workshop on development.[2]

> When everything comes from the outside, it is destructive. The money is cursed. If the money flows in like a river without control, the people go crazy (*se lancen como locos*). When everything comes from the outside and the project fails, who cares? Nowadays all the efforts are directed toward getting outside aid, but I believe that the most damaging thing is the abundance of money that comes from the outside. It is like an axe that divides the community. Everyone wants a piece of something that doesn't belong to them. But if we are working and sweating, our sweat supported by outside assistance can be good.

Padre Luis, thus, spoke to the point at issue. He had seen in his travels the destructive effects of aid flowing into a community where the people were not coherently addressing a clear plan for their own internal development. Yet, at the time, the same Padre Luis was using his international contacts to line up two large grants for Santa María. One, for $150,000, would be for cattle, to enable 130 families in the village each to get a cow, with the provision that each cow's first offspring would be given to the agricultural coop of the village to enable it to become a stronger agent for change. The other grant, for $165,000, would be for infrastructure development, including potable water for the population, a four-wheel-drive truck, reforestation, and training.

Thus, Padre Luis was strongly warning about the seductions of external funding while he was also working to bring in a major infusion of aid. In the juxtaposition of these two factors lay the contradictions of development in an area destroyed in one era and force-fed development later on. Padre Luis's bridging idea that "if we are working and sweating . . ." still begs the question of whether the laborers had the experience of seeing themselves as social subjects in Freire's sense of the term.

One indicator would be whether the community as such—apart from the singular vision that a man like Miguel Reyes brought— was able to take stock of the overall challenges to the future life of the community and plan appropriate options for dealing with them.

When asked how the community anticipated and planned for the future, Pedro Canil said that the most important body in that regard was the board of the cooperative. Every year, he said, the board set out a work plan for the year ahead. To a question about whether it planned five or ten years ahead, he said it did not. Life, then, unfolded from year to year. The question was whether that would be adequate to deal with the issues of alternative employment, deforestation, and possible despoiling of the land by the oil companies.

A hopeful long-term possibility lay in the lively educational process in Santa María described in the previous chapter. In 1997, three young women from the community were attending the national university. In October of that year, six young men graduated from a progressive secondary school in Guatemala City. They planned to go on to the university on scholarships provided by a U.S. denominational church group. Thirty-one students, many of them outstanding, would be graduating from the junior high, thirty of them with scholarships to attend high schools throughout the country. All of the scholarship recipients have committed themselves to return to the Ixcán to pursue their careers.

This level of exposure to ideas and the discipline of studying, together with the high commitment to education on the part of the community itself, will provide a framework and professional resources for the development of plans and initiatives for the future. And, given Santa María's increasing ties to the region through its schools, the village will have an impact beyond its boundaries as it sets its direction.

Ixcán Grande Cooperatives

The Ixcán Grande cooperatives, just to the north of Santa María, contrast sharply with Santa María with respect to development. Some analysis of the development path of this set of cooperative communities will illustrate the enormous complexity of development when crossfires of competing interests exist within a refugee return community.

The Ixcán Grande cooperatives were hardest hit in the scorched-earth campaign of 1982 and were an area of heavy conflict in subsequent years. Communities of population in resistance had settled on cooperative land (indeed, many people in CPRs had been members of the cooperatives), to some extent protected by the guerrillas, which resulted in the army making the area an ongoing target for its counterinsurgency campaign.

With the signing of the refugee accords in October 1992 and movement by the CPRs out of the cover of the forest to live openly, a sea change in the area was under way. Major groups of refugees returned from August through December 1993 to repopulate the former communities and to reestablish the cooperative structure that had existed before.

The Ixcán Grande cooperatives differed from the buying and selling cooperative in Santa María in that in the former the land itself was held cooperatively. Each of the five original communities in the area had its own cooperative, coordinated by representatives to a central group. Shortly after the 1982 violence, one of those five communities, Xalbal, came under army sway. Prior to the return of the refugees, Xalbal separated from the rest of the community, a process facilitated in part by the Roman Catholic bishop in the area, who helped settle complicated land issues.

Given the extensive nature of the returns and knowledge of the heroic struggle of the CPRs over the years, coupled with the ongoing armed conflict in the region, the Ixcán Grande attracted widespread attention. Accompaniers flocked in to offer international eyes and ears, as provided for in the October 1992 accords, and a variety of agencies moved in to distribute development funds.

As they had with other returns, the Permanent Commissions, made up of representatives of the various refugee camps in Mexico, arranged the logistics of the returns to Ixcán Grande. With the returns accomplished, however, their role became more complicated. One logical position the commissions could have taken, given their mandate did not necessarily extend beyond arranging the returns, would have been to disband. With that, they could have made way for the reestablishment of the elected cooperative structure, which had continued in a latent but recognized way while the refugees were in Mexico. Given human nature and bureaucratic momentum, however, that did not happen.

A further complicating factor was the behind-the-scenes role of the guerrillas, who had been active not only within Guatemala but also in Mexico, where they had been in dialogue with the refugee communities and their leaders. Several of the people interviewed were open about the fact that the guerrillas were a presence in Mexico, but they were very clear in saying that the armed resistance was in no way in control of decision-making processes among the refugee communities. The guerrillas had a point of view and argued it but couldn't impose it.

The refugee communities had evolved what developed into a strategic alliance with the guerrillas well before they fled to Mexico. Under the circumstances, it was the natural thing to do. The army was the agent that had destroyed their villages and massacred their friends and relatives. Those awakened to the wider context of their lives knew that, although the army was a power in its own right, it also protected the privilege of the economic elite. Together, this powerful coalition oppressed the poor, including the refugees. In the hurricane of increasing violence leading up to the scorched-earth campaign, the guerrillas and the population interacted, developing mutually reinforcing positions. The strategic alliance, thus, was between the armed guerrillas and the civilian population. The latter agreed with many of the positions of the guerrillas, without having to agree that armed struggle was the way to achieve commonly held goals.

As the Permanent Commissions looked to expand their role, the northwest group, which included the Ixcán Grande cooperatives, decided to break the strategic alliance with the guerrillas. On the one hand, an influential figure in the break was a disaffected former guerrilla commander who lobbied the Permanent Commissions to sever their ties with the revolutionary group he had quit. On the other hand, the leaders of the cooperative directorate maintained their historic alliance. As a result, the unity in the return community of the Ixcán Grande cooperatives, so crucial to its development, came unraveled (NCOORD 1996).

In the context of an ongoing civil war, people with the best of intentions can come to opposing views regarding the best way to increase pressure to sign peace agreements. Armed struggle, at least until a definitive peace is signed, is one option. Others could logically conclude that, given the changed situation in the world, with the ending of the Cold War, armed struggle was no longer viable. An alternative option would be to seek negotiated solutions, taking advantage of all available development resources. A consideration for some in this thought process was their disillusionment with the way the guerrillas had appeared to let them down, or the way the guerrillas had used money without adequate accountability.

Unfortunately, good will was in short supply in the Ixcán Grande. The Permanent Commissioners, in particular, adopted a highly conflictual and aggressive method for furthering their aims. Having broken with the guerrillas, they sought to become independent development brokers for the area. They had the legitimacy of being the named figures on the refugee side in the 1992 accords and used it to position themselves and get resources vis-à-vis development agencies.

As self-appointed development brokers, the Permanent Commissioners found themselves in conflict with the leaders of the Ixcán Grande cooperatives. In the face-off, the commission-aligned leaders moved by using persistent and, by most accounts, bullying tactics to take over the leadership of the entire Ixcán Grande structure. In the process, they accused people who didn't agree with them of being with the guerrillas, a very serious charge, particularly before the signing of the peace accords. Once in control, one of their early actions was to deny the CPRs an area of land on which they could continue their communal lifestyle. The CPRs were then forced to relocate to a new area.

Padre Beto described his view of the role of the Permanent Commissioners in development:

> According to what I have heard, they have changed their vision of development. In place of some concept of integral development that is liberating, of promoting the interests of all the communities and for the people, theirs is now more in the line of developmentalism (*desarrollismo*). It is within the framework of neoliberal capitalism. They had to have a total of four meetings with the people of Pueblo Nuevo [one of the cooperatives] to pressure them to let the oil company people in. . . . The directors of the Ixcán Grande cooperatives [prior to the

takeover by the people aligned with the Permanent Commissioners] had been opposed to the entry of the oil company, for all it signifies, including damage to the environment (interview, November 1995).

So development, far from an expression of the internal initiative of the whole community, became the publicly stated goal of one aggressive faction.

Following the signing of the peace accords, in December 1996, the conflict took another turn toward social volatility and violence. One of those accords provided for the demobilization of the former guerrilla combatants. When the demobilized tried to return to the community, they were threatened with violence. The cooperative members then voted to take the land rights away from those who had demobilized. In a related action, the members of the women's group Mama Maquin were accused of having ties to the URNG and the group's building was burned to the ground. The decision to bar the ex-guerrillas was constitutionally illegal, and a variety of entities, including those who were barred, determined to reverse the decision. The inevitable outcome, however, was a rupture in the community that would take a long time to heal (Long 1997, 10–12).

Although the returnees in this case had the potential to challenge the army's control in the area, the return population turned on itself internally. The hope and energy generated from the human rights training and the determination to reweave life within the country was dissipated. In this context, the huge challenge for the future lay with the returnees to find common ground on their essential interests.

Perils of Development: Experience of the Agencies

The people from the development agencies who were interviewed, to a person, had a positive view of the role they and their agencies were playing in the development of the Ixcán region. They knew the buzzwords and could use them in the perspective of their work. Nothing surprising in that. But in the flow of continuous questioning, other, often less positive, issues surfaced.

One chance conversation with a zone inspector for a Guatemalan agency, the Social Investment Fund (FIS in Spanish), brought to the surface underlying problems in his outlook. He described the goal of

FIS to help people become productively independent, for which, he said, the people needed to diversify their agricultural products. When asked if his agency worked to understand and integrate with the culture of the people, he said no—not as an agency, though he had done some reading as an individual. Then he said, "The people don't have an authentic culture. They are pulled by the revolutionary left and the military right, so they have no center" (interview, November 1995).

The implication was that the people he had in mind couldn't be counted on to develop themselves from within while drawing on resources from outside agencies to help them reach their goals. The first step, then, was for the agency to help the villagers become independent economically, by enabling them to have something viable to sell. Presumably, as they became more viable economically, they would evolve a more authentic culture—in the global economy, the only internationally recognized "valid" one.

In an extensive interview with staff people from Centro Canadiense de Estudios y Cooperación Internacional (CECI), a Canadian agency with U.N. funding, two people, Walter Robles and Danilo Hub, spoke about their philosophy of development. Theirs was a large agency, which worked in ninety-three countries, principally in development. Robles, a staff person working out of the headquarters of the agency in Guatemala City, went right to the heart of the matter. "The philosophy of CECI," he said, "is precisely one of integral development, based in the participation of the person who is involved in her/his development" (interview, November 1995).

Robles went on to make a sophisticated distinction between integral development and quick-impact projects, which are of short duration—three months to a year—and financed by the UNHCR and administered by CECI. These include such small projects as obtaining corn mills, cardamom dryers, and trucks to get products to market. These projects are the building blocks that enable a community to get started, but they are not yet development, which takes place over the longer term. Quick-impact projects are intended to be bridges to development.

When asked how the philosophy worked on a daily basis, he said:

> We, as an institution, have our philosophy of work. This is to initiate
> with the community meetings in which we work, on the one hand, for

the participation of the whole group, not only men or women, but an assembly in which everyone participates, and in this assembly we begin to speak regarding the needs of the community. On the other hand, we begin to assign priorities to these needs. What are the most important needs? . . . And we try to be sure that the project has a strong training component, partly related to administration, with another part related to the technical aspects of the project.

CECI recognized that it would be in a community for only a short time and did not take over the management of projects. It worked through regional groups, such as the area association of health promoters, to get them involved.

CECI recognized as well, Robles said, the importance of working with both returnees and those who stayed. In this regard, he referred to a project to build corn mills in Santa María, where initially there were the two women's groups. Policy, he said, prohibited them from doing any project with one group or the other, so the agency invested time over a couple of months until the women agreed to work together.

What Robles described sounded like an enlightened framework from headquarters, and, indeed, people from Santa María had good things to say about CECI. Pedro Canil described the agency's work this way:

> They work well with us, because when they were thinking to do these projects [he had been describing their work with the cardamom drier, the corn mills, and the truck], they came to us to hear what the people were saying. Are they in agreement? So they came to participate with us. And the people said it is good to provide these projects. This is what CECI has done. What they still plan to give us is a group of chickens, but that hasn't come yet. And they will leave after that, according to what they say (interview, November 1995).

Padre Beto had another take on development agencies, including CECI. He said that all too often the agencies imposed projects on a community. "They have little projects," he said, "always the same— latrines, schools—because they don't have greater capacity." For Padre Beto, that kind of help, while useful, didn't get to the heart of the people-centered development that was needed (interview, November 1995).

The views of the CECI staff, of Pedro Canil, and of Padre Beto all can be reconciled as accurately reflecting reality. CECI staff do meet with the people to ask their opinions but do so with particular projects in mind. From that perspective, the people logically feel heard and have the sense that the agency is working with them. At the same time, the very participatory nature of the process can divert attention from the community's need to do its own self-assessments and planning as a base from which to decide whether the CECI projects fit in to the community's self-defined direction.

The crux of the matter was whether the people had come together within their own decision-making processes and with enough of a sense of community autonomy to generate the momentum and power to carry on with development after the agencies left. With that end in mind, the training CECI described was necessary but not yet sufficient. The issue was whether the community itself had internal coherence and a sense of itself as what Freire calls the "historical subject," capable of taking history into its own hands and shaping it with the resources at its disposal.

Resources for Reweaving: The Stakes Are High

Benito Morales, a church worker from Guatemala City who had been to the Ixcán many times on assignment from a religious agency, sketched a sobering prophecy of what was happening to the area where Santa María and the Ixcán Grande cooperatives are located. He described the neoliberal world economy, which dogmatically required support for the corporate private sector and cut resources to the poor, as an avalanche that no one could stop. The only choice was to deal with it, and the question was how to attack it with as much organization and insight—internal development—as possible.

In the neoliberal world economy, the role of a country like Guatemala was to provide cheap agricultural commodities and very low-wage labor for finishing industries. In Latin America, the latter were referred to as *maquilas* and involved people working at starvation wages assembling parts for clothing, small electronic items, and so on, which were then shipped to consumer economies in the north.

Morales described his concerns about the Ixcán, which included both the extraction of its oil and the introduction of maquilas:

> I have no doubt there will be maquilas imposed in the Ixcán. So there will be some planning going on to introduce them to the area. But because the Ixcán, together with the Petén, are on the border with Mexico, it is strategically vital for commercial interests that the borders be open. There may be some time for delay and resistance, during which time those who sense what is happening can inform the rest, but finally the area will be integrated into the neoliberal production system, including both the oil wells and the maquilas (interview, November 1995).

A year and a half later, noting the divisions in the Ixcán Grande, Morales had an even more guarded prognosis for the future in the Ixcán:

> With all the divisions, it will be even harder for the people to resist. The vocation of the land in the Ixcán is not agriculture but forest. But the people are still using it for agriculture and subsistence. If the people don't find alternatives that fit the area, the soil will be exhausted, and they will have to leave again or find other commercial ventures on the border. . . . If the people can't solve their divisions, they will turn internally to families and personal problems, with no ear to hear what is happening in the rest of the area or the world (interview, June 1997).

But, he said, organizers had to keep creative and dreaming of a better world. They would have to scramble in the relatively brief transition time—before the wave of development agencies left and the new global economic order settled in—to gain as much advantage as possible in terms of educating folks and developing alternative sources of income. For the people to pursue the kind of liberation Morales had in mind, they would have to make substantial progress in understanding the world system and in developing the internal competence and confidence necessary to take advantage of the scarce resources available.

The urgency of the oil issue was evident in a report issued on July 20, 1996, in which research indicated a probable reserve of 740 million barrels of oil in the Ixcán region. The Triton Oil Company was scheduled to introduce wells in January 1997. As of June

1997, however, the first well was just being installed but pumping had not yet begun (interview, Dan Long, June 1997).

The challenge for the returnees and for those who stayed, given the perils of development, was enormous. Losing would mean, if Morales was right, that many proud Maya campesinos, who defined themselves in relation to their communities and land, would become humiliated, exploited laborers in the maquilas and toil in fields where the land was less and less productive as it exhausted its nutrients.

Conclusion

This chapter has explored three types of development: first, people-centered development, which generates from the internal vision of a community and enables its members to take their own initiatives, based on their own self-defined needs; second, agency-initiated development, which flows from the views of funding sources and may or may not engage people's own vision and initiatives; and third, corporate-initiated development, based in the private sector and the global economy. Summarizing the three in reverse order, the global economy provided the dominant framework within which the Guatemalan government of President Arzú sought to be a player. Its program was described in Chapter 3 as privatizing the economy in all essential respects except security. For the latter, the military and the police remained prominent actors. Private property was to be protected in the interests of the powerful, including the large land owners. Development in the Ixcán, including in Santa María Tzejá and the Ixcán Grande, took place in that broad context.

Development is often seen as the province of development agencies of the kind that provide resources for projects that benefit local communities. The list in this chapter of such projects included latrines, wells for potable water, corn mills, and the like—all of which provided undeniable benefits to the communities involved but did not touch on the larger structural issues of land ownership and the way resources flow through society. Agencies varied in their commitment to work with and to empower communities. Alianza was one agency that sought to encourage the people to develop a vision and initiative. PRODESSA, noted for its educational work in

Santa María, was another. Other agencies were less committed to the form of development that took shape in the participating lives of the communities.

The baseline for development, as Alianza and PRODESSA recognized, was people-centered, whereby local communities acted as "social subjects," as the agents of their own development. From the base of their own self-understanding and identity, their own culture, and their own vision, plans, and initiative, communities draw on projects of the agencies and indeed the resources of the nation. In contrast to the privatized global economy, this is a democratized local economy.

A central problem for the returnees was that they were not well prepared to confront the hard world of development in their communities. Their strong desires in this regard were constrained by more traditional visions or, as in the case of the Ixcán Grande, by competing, even self-destructive strategies. Given the likely short period of development agency work in the area and the impinging oil, wood, and maquila agendas of the world economy, the challenge for people-centered development was formidable. Meeting the challenge would require heightened efforts on the part of local leaders, agencies, and churches that shared in this vision.

People-centered development would mean, ultimately, centering on and nurturing cultural resources like the education offered in Santa María schools and by PRODESSA. It would mean fostering consciousness of the world economic order but from the perspective of the critical importance of Maya and campesino unity. It would mean planning first to use the internal resources of the community and looking outward for help only when sweat equity was clearly in place. And it would mean, following Freire, that the people would not be the objects of someone else's hurried idea of imposed development but rather become the subjects of their own integral development, building from the values of their own culture to shape their own future.

CHAPTER SIX

Human Rights
The Color of Life

> As we prepared for the return to Guatemala, there were many
> courses . . . especially to prepare human rights promoters. And we
> began to study the Guatemalan constitution to learn what it said.
> Before that we had read it somewhat but had never analyzed what
> it meant. But in those workshops we began to study exactly what the
> constitution says.

> —Returnee to Santa María

ALTHOUGH THE returnees had come back to Guatemala
with little preparation for dealing with the complexities
they would face in the area of development, they had been inundated
with information and training regarding their rights. The returnee
quoted above described the workshops given to leaders selected to
become human rights promoters. He also told how, at least in his
return group, all those planning to go back met at four o'clock every
afternoon for talks related to the return. Some of those talks were
about human rights, with an emphasis on treating those who stayed
with full respect, given that their experiences were so different (interview, November 1995).

After the joy of being reunited with family members and friends,
the returnees confronted the clash of patterns described in Chapter 4.
One major contrast between the groups was the preparation each
had regarding human rights. Whereas the refugees had studied the
constitution and international human rights documents, those who
stayed had been conditioned by the military authorities in the area to
view the concept of human rights with high suspicion, to understand
human rights as a wedge issue of the vilified guerrillas.

Nonetheless, within three years of the return, the village had been relatively successful in reweaving what had been so brutally torn, including in the complicated human rights arena. An initial effort to organize a human rights educational campaign gave way to a lower profile for the theme in the period following the signing of the peace accords. By then, the lack of immediate violations of rights in the local area led to a shift of attention to other areas, including the construction of new buildings and fascination with the high level of activity in the schools.

At the same time, a review of those first three years is important for the insight it provides into the way that the issue of human rights found its way into the reweaving process.

The Campaign for Human Rights in Santa María

In the first years after the refugees returned, Santa María became a fragile but emerging model for a holistic and just society in Guatemala. Harbingers of the new order included a core of educators, called human rights promoters, and the play *The Past Is with Us*, which depicted the history of the violence inflicted on the village from a human rights perspective. The very idea of having human rights promoters or a forthright play on a human rights theme would have been unthinkable before the return. The ongoing risks of involvement in the human rights arena were symbolized, however, by the terrifying experience of a young woman from the village who was threatened with violence in what seems to have been a thinly veiled threat to her father, an activist leader in the village.

At the urging of the returnees, the village named six people to serve as human rights promoters. One proudly noted at a meeting in November 1995 that they had been named "from the midst of the people"—implying that they had the full legitimacy of the community. Five promoters were men. Three were returnees, while the other three—significantly—were people who had stayed in the village while the refugees were in Mexico. All six human rights promoters were volunteers; they received no stipend for their work.

The six human rights promoters were named so the village would be represented in the Popular Organization for the Defense of Human Rights in Guatemala (OPODEDHGUA), a group originally formed among the refugees in Mexico. That an organization with that origin was attracting even a few of those who stayed was very important, indicating, as it did, that the reweaving process was moving forward. The three promoters who had stayed, however, were reported by the returnees to be the only ones in whom they had full confidence at that time.

The November 1995 meeting with the six promoters is worth summarizing here for the window it provides into the development of consciousness of human rights in the area. An analysis of what was said offers a basis for understanding the profound challenge the expansion of human rights consciousness posed to the control project of the army and the economic elites. The focus of the meeting was not only civil and political rights but economic rights—to housing and land.

An echo of the virulent racism that has pervaded Guatemalan society occurred early in the meeting, when the topic turned to human rights. "We are intelligent human beings, not savages," one person said. A short time later, someone said, "We are not savages, or animals." Several times outside the meeting people had said, "We deserve to be treated as human beings, not like little animals." That refrain revealed the framework indigenous and poor Guatemalans had been subjected to, and had partly internalized, before they came to know their rights.

The people at the meeting talked about rights documents they had studied, including the Global Accord on Human Rights, signed between the armed resistance (URNG) and the government in March 1994, and the constitution of Guatemala. "The constitution gives us our rights," they said. And, "We are using the constitution to demand our rights. What the constitution says, we will use." Indeed, the constitution of Guatemala was, on the whole, a progressive document as it was written. The problem lay not in what was written but in the reality that it had not been enforced, except selectively to benefit the rich.

When asked how they were defining human rights, the people at the meeting described the unfolding of inalienable rights through the life cycle, starting with the pregnant woman, who has rights to medical care and protection. When the baby is born, she/he is entitled to protection. Children, as they grow, have the right to education, to schools and teachers. As they get older, they have the rights of free speech, further education, and health care, and they can demand their rights.

"As campesinos," one villager said, "we have the right to land, but the most serious problem is that the government doesn't provide land, and they must do that. Since the government isn't fulfilling the rightful demands, people are protesting." Access to land, the most explosive issue in Guatemala, was thus named as a human right.

Women have equal rights with men. "We have the right to participate in meetings," the young woman in the group affirmed, "to have leadership posts, to study, to speak out, to organize, and the right to live without abuse." One of the men, however, noted both the ideal and the real situation. "We have an obligation to respect the rights of women. . . . But their voice is not respected. There is bad treatment. How can we speak with women without fighting? How do we learn?"

A major problem noted in the meeting was that people did not know what their rights were. The government authorized rights through the constitution, but people didn't know what they were or how to demand them. That was the role of promoters, they said, to pass information to people so they knew.

One of the men described what he and the others who stayed experienced during the twelve years the refugees were in Mexico. First, he said, he and the others didn't blame the refugees for fleeing. They were simply defending their lives. But, he said, the army had told those who stayed that the refugees were bad people—but those who stayed knew the refugees weren't.

The regional priest, he noted, had lifted the veil a bit by offering a workshop on human rights before the return. One of the main points was that the army had no right to enter their houses and drag them out—even if there was no door on the house, soldiers couldn't come in. But there were consequences for going to the workshop. After the few who went returned, they were threatened by the people who had taken over the land of the refugees in Santa María. When a subsequent meeting on human rights was held, the people in Santa María didn't go.

Then, when the refugees returned, the situation changed: "We could see each other and talk freely. Before, when we had military commissioners, they spoke; but we couldn't. When the return happened, a good change took place. We are now free. No one can ask for our identification papers. There are no checkpoints on the road. We aren't afraid to participate in human rights any longer."

However, not everyone felt the same way as these human rights promoters. One promoter reported a conversation he overheard at a birthday party: "They began to talk about all the meetings and the groups that work in the community. 'All that has come with the returnees. There are so many meetings. They come with tricks. We don't want them or their workshops. This idea of rights is to take away our rights. Only the military can protect us.'"

When asked how many villagers were in the hard-line group that supported the army, the promoters consulted among themselves. Perhaps only ten families, they said, directly represented the ideas of the army. The hard-liners reported the army's saying that "within three years, if the returnees and their supporters continue what they are doing, we [the army] will finish them off." The army responded, "Don't involve yourselves with the returnees. They talk of human rights, but that is of the guerrillas."

But although only ten families were in the hard-line resistance, many more among those who stayed still didn't know their rights and were fearful about getting involved. In interviews outside that meeting, the theme of fear as a reason not to become involved in working for human rights came up again and again. The most fearful people were those who stayed.

The work of these human rights promoters was at a preliminary stage, a fragile beginning. Forward movement was slowed by the fact that the leader of the group had suffered a serious accident, from which he was slow to recover. In August 1996, he was still convalescing but said he was eager to get on with the human rights education process. He emphasized that the community had to support the promoters in their work and that enthusiasm was lacking, but he was optimistic that the promoters would make an impact.

But although there was a substantial amount of fear in the community—well founded, given what the villagers had been through—Santa María was nevertheless a community on the move in the human rights arena, as the very existence of a group of human rights promoters attested. Another strong indicator was the play *The Past Is with Us*. One of its key dramatic themes was the naming of a series of articles in the Guatemalan constitution dealing with human rights, followed by the names of individuals murdered in the violence, whose deaths were evidence of the violation of the constitutional human rights articles. Teenaged actors boldly proclaimed what would have been suicidal statements before the return:

Second article of the Guatemalan constitution, duties of the state: It is the duty of the state to guarantee for all inhabitants of the republic life, liberty, security, peace and the integral development of each person.

> *Cristian Canil Suar, seven years old, and*
> *Eufrasia Canil Suar, fourteen years old*

Article 12 of the Guatemalan constitution: The right to defense: The defense of each person and their rights is inviolable. No one may be imprisoned or deprived of their rights without first having been summoned, heard, and convicted in a legal proceeding before the authorized judge or tribunal.

> *Eduardo Canil Vincente, thirteen years old,*
> *Maria Guadalupe Canil Vincente, nine years old, and*
> *Fedelia Vincente Mendoza, thirty years old*

Article 51 of the Guatemalan constitution: Protection of minors and the elderly: The state will protect the physical, mental, and moral health of minors and the elderly.

> *Sebastiana Cos, eighty-four years old,*
> *Estela Canil Vincente, four years old, and*
> *Graciela Canil Vincente, seven months old*

Perhaps for the soldiers, those who died weren't anybody. But for us they were our loved ones, our sons and daughters, our mothers and fathers, our brothers and sisters. We have the right to say the truth! They were all very good people, and it was unjust that the soldiers killed them, that the soldiers took away their right to life.

The play is extraordinary in a number of ways. First, it was developed as part of a theater competition on human rights themes and staged for the first time in front of an audience that included army people—who themselves entered a play in the competition. Second, the play served publicly to link human rights vividly to the Guatemalan constitution. Third, it was acted by young people, who themselves experienced vicariously the horrendous violation of rights that their parents suffered and that they, themselves, endured as small children.

This play, along with the existence and work of the human rights promoters, was evidence in the period following the return that the human rights challenge was being aggressively addressed in Santa María. One of the human rights promoters spoke of the determination they brought to the work:

> We are participating, practicing. We want to move forward, and we are going to have security for the people, regardless of what happens. . . . So we are preparing workshops, courses, and we are giving service regarding this theme to everyone. I am giving my time, not only for me but for all the people that may need help here, so we can work together. . . . But the way I see it, little by little we will get there (interview, November 1995).

Clearly, the human rights promoters worked energetically, took risks to ensure human rights, and created a climate of hope that rights would be ensured within the village, but the experience of calling on a young woman from Santa María who was detained in the capital at gunpoint emphasized how much was at stake. At the age of seventeen, she had been sent by her father to study nursing in a Guatemala City hospital.

On her way home one day, she was shadowed by a man wearing military-issue boots but who was otherwise in civilian clothes. He followed her to a point very near her house and watched her enter. Within a week, two other men, similarly dressed, positioned themselves on either side of her as she waited for her bus. One of them opened his jacket to reveal a pistol. They told her not to run or cry out and to get on a bus with them. As they rode, they said they knew who her father was and questioned her about his activities. Some time later, they got off the bus with her and allowed her to leave, with a warning that she should tell no one. She called her father, however, who asked the Needham church delegation, visiting at the time, to go to where she was staying to give her support.

This story illustrates how those involved in effective leadership roles that involve organizing for rights not only risk their own lives but put the lives of their loved ones in danger. It indicated, also, that the reach of the security forces and their sources of information continued to be extensive and detailed. The terror was not what it was in the early 1980s, but it continued to be selective, with sufficient intensity to keep those working for justice constantly fearful and on guard. Space for the expression of human rights in Guatemala would not be won cheaply.

Nonetheless, all of the human rights activities demonstrated that the returnees to Santa María and their increasing base of allies among those who stayed were working to make the village a model on the human rights front. The ideal was still far off, as the tensions between returnees and those who stayed played out along the fault line described in Chapter 4. But residents in the village already had some critical insight regarding development as a human right and were moving to educate the community through an active group of human rights promoters.

At the end of the three-year period following the return of the refugees, the theater group that produced *The Past Is with Us* was still active and touring. By June 1996, the play had toured nine communities, including some that had been decimated by the massacres. Parts of the play have been filmed by Canadian and British (BBC) filmmakers. Randall Shea, the director, reports that the work has been refined continuously, most recently in May 1997, making it even more powerful. In June 1997, the play toured again, with thirteen performances, including three in Guatemala City. Through this vehicle, Santa María has been educating the nation and world about the power of human rights to transform society.

Although the specific activities of the human rights promoters were reduced after three years, the lead human rights promoter, Gaspar Quino, along with two or three others, continued to attend regional workshops and hoped to revive the work of the promoters. At the same time, several women reported that they held a series of workshops dealing with women's rights. As with the training for the general population, the training for women on this theme had begun in Mexico. Then, after the return, nearly all the women had attended workshops on women's rights, offered by the office of the ombudsman for human rights, by the United Nations, and by various agencies.

An important additional source of understanding about human rights was the educational program offered in the schools. The curriculum, stimulated by PRODESSA, dealt with human rights from a variety of perspectives, including the rights of women, indigenous peoples, and general citizens. The play *The Past Is with Us*, performed by students as part of their learning, emphasizes the way rights were violated during the violence. As students come back from progressive educational institutions at the secondary and university levels, they bring reinforcement regarding human rights and the importance of protecting them. In August 1997, three young men trained under PRODESSA auspices at a high school in the capital were in the village doing their teaching internships, working directly in the classrooms (author observation in Santa María).

Two more factors were at play that promised the villagers exposure to human rights issues. One was the rising tide of awareness about the content of the peace accords. Although the government appeared distracted from the accords and intent on its global economy agenda, groups in the civilian society were undertaking educational campaigns around the accords, which included the important accord on human rights. One such group was the coalition of indigenous groups, COPMAGUA, with its lead group, Defensoría Maya. Other groups included the coalition of women's groups and the coalition of campesino organizations. These coalitions were increasingly active in reaching out to the rural areas. Another important actor in the human rights arena was the Roman Catholic church. The second important source of human rights exposure was the network of human rights organizations in the Ixcán, the theme of the next section.

Strengthening Human Rights in the Ixcán

With the return of the refugees, active human rights organizations in the Ixcán came to public attention. Two groups had been formed in the area prior to the return but had had low profiles. One of these was a network of human rights groups among the communities of populations in resistance, while the other was a small group founded among people who had stayed in Guatemala in the villages. With the return, the refugees brought the association of human rights promoters, OPODEDHGUA, the group the promoters in Santa María were part of. These three groups made up the Ixcán Regional Human Rights Alliance (CORDHI).

The three CORDHI groups arose out of very different circumstances, but when representatives of these groups began to share what they were doing, they discovered they had similar objectives: "Demilitarization, the defense of human rights, the strengthening of Maya culture and the promotion of community organizations and political participation." In July 1995, they opened an office in Cantabal, staffed by volunteers, two at a time, from each of the three agencies (Rader 1997, 61).

CORDHI offered a range of workshops, using the style of popular education, in as many communities as it could find the interest. Its strategy was to draw participants into dialogue about what they had experienced and how they should be treated as human beings. The quotation above offers a succinct appraisal of their educational stance. According to CORDHI, popular education was defined as follows:

> Popular education is not about knowledge per se, rather it is a process rooted in a critical analysis of one's own lived experience and observations. It stresses the intimate connection between education and activism and encourages participants to become protagonists in their own lives. Joined with an analysis of human rights, it becomes a vehicle for reconciliation, community organization and political organization: a strong foundation for a democratic political culture (Rader 1997, 65).

The Roman Catholic church in the area sponsors a human rights program for lay teachers, or catechists, through its Catholic Office for Human Rights in the Ixcán (OCADHI). Padre Beto Ghiglia is the coordinator and guiding spirit. He described the work prior to the signing of the peace accords as focused on human rights more traditionally conceived. But although that aspect continued after the December 1996 signing of the accords, the emphasis by June 1997 had shifted: "Perhaps now the challenge is to address economic, social, and political rights. And there is more: the right of the environment, of creation, and the right to solidarity. And the right of communities to their own development and their own identity" (interview, June 1997).

In the highly militarized Ixcán region, where control by the army had been nearly complete, the climate shifted following the refugees' return. People found new freedom, in part stimulated by the returnees and the people in CPRs, to speak out and claim their rights. The energy came from within the communities to which the refugees returned, to be sure, but when it flagged there, as it did for a time in Santa María, it could be replenished from human rights initiatives taken by CORDHI and the church at the regional level. In any case, the lively colors of human rights were finding their way into the reweaving of the torn in the Ixcán.

The Threat Human Rights Pose to the Ruling Elites

The Guatemalan constitution, which provides legitimation for the army and the government, is very progressive on human rights. Article 2, as noted in *The Past Is with Us*, defines the duties of the state as "to guarantee to residents of the republic life, liberty, justice, security, peace, and the integral development of the person." The next 132 articles deal with human rights under two chapters, Individual Rights and Social Rights, beginning with the right to life (Article 3). The third section, under Social Rights, deals with indigenous communities, in which the government is committed to protect ethnic groups and their lands, including providing loans for their development. Article 118 states that the economic and social regimen of the Republic of Guatemala "is based on the principle of social justice."

From the perspective of the army and the economic elites prior to the signing of the firm and final peace accords, these articles were explosive material. If the constitutional text was to be enforced, the rulers' project for controlling the poor—more than three-quarters of the population—was doomed. That, precisely, was the threat posed by the returning refugees, who said, "We use the constitution"— that is, we base our campaign for justice on that document. Further, the returnees knew that the basis for joining economic rights with the rest of human rights was written in as a subpart of Title II of the constitution, which deals with individual and social rights.[1]

The position of the army was made further vulnerable, in an abstract sense at least, by the documents they had been a party to in the peace process, including the Global Accord on Human Rights, the Accord on the Rights of Indigenous Peoples, and the Accord on Land and Economic Issues.

The overall problem faced by the guardians of the status quo was that the language in these documents was strong. Repressive actions violating the provisions had the potential to render the perpetrators guilty in the court of world opinion if a clear enough spotlight could be brought to bear in the international media. That held a potentially greater threat than what might happen in the dysfunctional legal system of Guatemala.

Given the absolute quicksand it stood on in its legal position, the army had only one recourse, to block implementation of the constitution itself, which provided the very legal basis for the army's existence. That meant, as a first order of defense, keeping people ignorant of the provisions and badly educated enough that they were unlikely to discover constitutional provisions on their own. The second line of defense was to generate sufficient fear among the population to prevent even those who had some knowledge of human rights from pursuing those rights. The third line was more complex: to demonize, divide, and demoralize those who had both knowledge of human rights and the will to demand their rights. The fourth line, to be avoided if possible, was raw oppression—violence.

It is in this context that the returning refugees, with their knowledge of the constitution and their willingness to use it, represented such a threat. By mid-1997, thirty thousand refugees had already crossed the border in some eighteen organized return groups and individual repatriations (phone interview, Curt Wands, June 1997). From the army's perspective, it was already too late to keep the returnees in ignorance—knowledge was out of the bag. Fear as a deterrent also had limited force, given the returnees' determination not to submit to army repression and dominance. That left only the third and fourth lines of defense.

Demonize, Divide, and Demoralize— and Kill if Necessary

Before the refugees returned to Santa María, fear had been pervasive. The old-timers lived in constant anxiety that the newcomers would go to the base to denounce them as communists or guerrillas. Even when a few people learned about human rights at the workshop offered by the priest, they didn't return for the follow-up. The majority of people knew little about human rights and were afraid to seek knowledge about them. Prior to the returns, then, the army's first two lines of defense against the "infection" of human rights education were successful.

Efforts to demonize the guerrillas and human rights went hand in hand. Army reeducation propaganda campaigns relentlessly repeated the contention that the violence had been caused by the guerrillas. Yes, the army might admit it had burned some villages and killed some people, but that had been necessary to cleanse the country of communists/subversives/terrorists (the term used depended on the prevailing ideology of international discourse, primarily defined by the U.S. State Department). Had it not been for the guerrillas, the army argued, the violence would not have been necessary. It was correct in the very limited sense that if the guerrillas hadn't fought for a more just society, the army wouldn't have launched the scorched-earth policy designed to depopulate the Ixcán and parts of the highlands in order to eliminate the guerrillas. But the army argument failed to acknowledge the centuries of structural violence designed to enlarge and protect the interests of economic elites and their army allies.

On the other side of the ledger, the guerrillas had gained a substantial following based on their analysis of the country's extreme economic polarization and repression. However, some of their tactics left a lingering negative impression. Occasionally, the guerrillas had killed civilians they judged to be traitors to their cause. The number of such killings was very small in comparison to those inflicted by the army, but they were remembered, particularly in the context of army propaganda. And the guerrillas had not always been fully open in accounting for money received from populations that supported them. But the major negative message left by the guerrilla campaigns was their inability to arm and defend the people who supported them and their subsequent abandonment of whole populations to the scorched-earth policy of the army.

A friend who lived in Guatemala for some time argued that the army won the propaganda war, and he was right. The military's nearly complete dominance of rural Guatemala gave the army control of the messages and images that entered the thinking of people subject to their control. The military's threat and selective use of violent repression gave authority to its position. And its position was that the guerrillas were enemies of the state and, more, were the embodiment of evil (demons). Association with them was tantamount to betrayal of the country, treason. To be named as one with ties to the guerrillas was to be put on a death list, made a target.

From demonizing the guerrillas, it was a short step to demonizing the whole concept of human rights. Again and again, interviewees reported the army saying that human rights were "of the guerrillas." One man reported that the only rights the army referred to prior to the return was the right of the people to defend their villages through participation in the army-organized civil patrols. The one right lifted from the constitution was the right to bear arms, again a reference to army-issued and army-controlled weapons to the civil patrols. Any rights beyond these were linked to the guerrillas and to be avoided, in effect, as life threatening (interview, Dan Long, June 1997).

Likewise, the refugees in Mexico were demonized by association with the guerrillas. That the refugees were learning about human rights in a massive way was not lost on the military. The military defense was to tar the refugees and human rights with the same brush—their ties to the demon guerrillas. People said they were told that the refugees were "bad people" whose heads had been filled with foreign ideas. Those who stayed were told not to get involved with refugee organizations, with the threat that if they did they would be inviting the return of the violence of 1982.

This demonizing of the refugees would carry only so far, however. With the actual return and the returnees at hand, the horns and other features ascribed to the demons fell away. Miguel Reyes described it this way:

> More than anything, the people [who stayed in Guatemala] had a great difference in their thinking, owing to the fact that in all that time the army was infusing the thinking of the people who stayed here that all of us who were in Mexico were guerrillas. And we were going to come from there and attack. So the people in Guatemala feared the refugees. They almost believed that we were people with horns. We were guerrillas. We were hairy creatures. Garbage. But it is not the case. For this reason, the people in Guatemala did not trust us. But little by little, it changed, particularly with the first returns (interview, November 1995).

With the returnees back and interweaving their lives with those who stayed, the demonizing strategy lost much of its effect. In Santa María, where the reintegration of the returnees was quite successful, the army lost ground. In fact, a local priest described Santa María as "lost territory" to the army, which "would not want any more Santa Marías."

But if demonizing lost its impact when the returnees took up life with those who stayed, the fallback strategy for the army was to separate the returnees from those who stayed. Let the refugees come back, if there was no other course—given the agreements and the pressure of world opinion—but let them settle in separate areas. That was the outcome in San Antonio Tzejá, a couple of villages to the south of Santa María.

In San Antonio Tzejá, the army's strategy was to work indirectly through the proxy organization ARAP-KSI. The evidence of the role of the proxy group is circumstantial but substantial. The case stems from a framework similar to that followed in Santa María. And, as in Santa María, the army invited in campesinos to take over land vacated by those who fled to Mexico. Some of the original settlers were part of the repopulation, though the proportion was not as high as in Santa María. The story told in this chapter emphasizes human rights issues.

The proxy group leading the resistance to the return to San Antonio was organized to resist the return to a number of villages. Its leader, Raúl Martínez, lived in a village called Kaibil Balam. Martínez organized civil patrol members in nearby villages to seek permanent titles to the land they occupied.

The link from defending the land to resisting the refugees was an easy one to make, given that people from the several towns had an interest in keeping the land out of messy negotiations with the returnees, in which they might lose out. The occupants didn't trust the government to give them an acceptable alternative. In an area with a dysfunctional legal system, where the army was the "law," the occupants took matters into their own hands and threatened the returnees with violence if they chose to return. In the process, the occupants violated a number of laws, including the taking of hostages.

When the San Antonio returnees decided to march to their land in defiance of the threats, they were accompanied by five people representing the United Nations and other international organizations. The five were brazenly taken hostage for a day, an egregious affront to the international community. As the hostages were detained, the members of Martínez's group shouted that they were *defending their rights*, a distorted theft of human rights language and a blind denial of the possibility that they might be denying the rights of their captives. The five hostages were released the next day, in the face of pressure that embarrassed the government. But even then Martínez, now an outlaw with nine warrants out for his arrest and an embarrassment to his country internationally, was allowed to carry on as leader of his group. In this militarized zone, his avoidance of arrest was ample evidence that he was protected and supported by the army (Tovar-Siebentritt 1996).

In negotiations that followed, the returnees were permitted to enter an area of their town's overall land mass but had to settle in a newly created center some distance from the then-existing center. The effect was to create two villages within the one village land area and to divide the two populations. In the new community, called Los Cimientos de la Nueva Esperanza (Foundations of New Hope), lived a population that had learned about human rights in Mexico. But they were separated from the villagers who had stayed, who continued to be under the control of the army. In this way, the population "infected" by human rights, as defined in the constitution, the

Global Accord on Human Rights, and the Universal Declaration of Human Rights, was effectively, if only temporarily, sealed off from the army-dominated part of the population.

Other communities in the area, including Raúl Martínez's home village of Kaibil Balam, have been allowed to defy and resist returns by refugees. In this way, the army, through the apparent use of a proxy, has been successful in avoiding any other "Santa María Tzejás." Human rights as a threat to army control have thus been contained, marginalized.

The last line of military defense against human rights—raw violence—has had its day as well. On October 5, 1995, an army patrol of twenty-six soldiers and an officer entered the returned refugee community of Aurora Ocho de Octubre (Aurora, Eighth of October—for the date on which the community was founded, just less than a year earlier), also known as Xamán, for the name of the farm where the community was located. The army was patrolling within the land area of the village, itself a provocative act, given the animosity villagers had for the military. When the residents learned of the army presence, they demanded to know why the patrol was there and called for the U.N. watchdog group MINUGUA to deal with the situation. When villagers challenged the soldiers to put their weapons down, the patrol fired on the crowd, killing eleven and wounding many others.

Was the massacre premeditated? MINUGUA determined that it probably was not. But clearly a climate had been created in which the army unit was predisposed to think of the returnees as the enemy and as subversive. And this was a community that could be seen as successful in reintegrating its residents. The Xamán farm had been purchased for the returnees, but people were already living on it who had been field workers for the previous owners. Rather than forcing them to leave, the returnees invited them to join in forming a new community. In its nearly full year of operation, the village had been moving forward effectively toward its goals.

Was a message intended in the harassment the army brought by its uninvited presence? Very likely. And certainly the message of the massacre itself was strong and clear. Many Guatemalan refugees still in Mexico were given pause about whether it was safe to return, in light of the Xamán massacre. The army, thus, was not averse to using its ultimate line of defense, savage violence, against the successful infusion of human rights.

In the post–peace accord period, the army was recreating its image. By the terms of the Accord on the Role of the Army in a Democratic Society, the army lost a third of its numbers and a third of its budget. But structural inequities remained, with racism and poverty the dominant forces in the democratic society the army was to protect from external forces. Would the past be prologue?

Conclusion

When Cesar Díaz, director of Alianza, was asked, with regard to the human rights network in the Ixcán, "Is it large enough to have impact, or is it only a seed?" he said:

> I believe it is a seed, but a vigorous seed. And if we see it in the context of the Ixcán, it is much more significant, much more significant. That is an isolated zone, with a huge military presence, with a recent experience of violence, where the return has made a great difference. This is a result of the return. If it weren't for the returnees, there wouldn't be any change in the Ixcán (interview, November 1995).

In his view, then, the work was just getting under way, but it was extremely important and a direct result of the refugees' return.

A year and a half later, the environment for human rights had changed significantly. With the peace accords signed and implementation under way, more people felt free to speak about human rights, at least at superficial levels, as evidenced by the network of human rights organizations that were operating in the region. The army was reducing its size and assuming a new public image. The vigorous seed Cesar Diaz described was growing.

But there were countertendencies as well. In the Ixcán Grande, the returnee population was rent down the middle, and each faction was violating the other's rights. In one moment the dominant group blocked the people in the CPRs, who had lived so courageously on the land during the period of army control, from taking contiguous land. In May 1997, that group had tried to expel ex-URNG militants when they demobilized. In Victoria, the original return community, the returnees were equally divided. Several communities that neighbored Santa María had successfully blocked refugees from returning to their former villages, and the occupants were close to receiving permanent titles to land.

Yet, even in these settings, where divisions sapped the energy that should have gone into healing and where injustice seemed to have its way, balancing factors, signs of hope, were in evidence. In the midst of high tension, neither the CPRs nor the demobilized guerrillas turned to violence to force their way. The CPRs moved to other land. The demobilized turned to legal routes and political pressure to claim their lands. Teams from the Organization of American States were moving quietly from one community to the other where the tensions were greatest, carefully listening to people and looking for common ground.

In the Santa María subregion called the Zona Reyna, the communities that had blocked returns had stabilized, and the returnees were seeking or had relocated to other lands. And, as noted in Chapter 4, the Santa María junior high school had become a meeting place for students and their parents who at first wanted nothing to do with the returnees or the returnees' conceptions of human rights but had come to work together on joint school-related improvements. The school's outreach, its curriculum, and its theater program all helped create an improved climate for human rights.

Underlying all these changes was the signal fact that the armed conflict was over. The guerrillas had demobilized and returned to their home communities or places of their choosing. The URNG nationally had recreated itself as a political party. And to the relief of the population, the army no longer flew overhead in helicopters or marched through to show its flag and force.

So the climate for human rights had changed. But whether human rights would begin to flourish for the long term was an open question. Inequities remained. Further, Guatemala still had no functioning judicial system or a mature police force to make the country's relatively progressive constitution a reality.

CHAPTER SEVEN

The Gray of Frozen Grief

Resolving the Trauma of Memory

Plan for extermination:
Raze the grass, tear out the roots of the last living plant,
Strew the earth with salt.
Afterwards, kill the memory of the grass.
In order to colonize consciousness, suppress it;
In order to suppress it, empty it of the past.
Annihilate all testimony that in that place there was
     ever something other
          than silence, prisons, and tombs.
It is forbidden to remember.

— Galeano, *Days and Nights of Love and War*

As a health promoter, I realize that possibly there are sicknesses that
don't need medicine. . . . The violence that happened here has left a
great deal of damage in the heart of each person. It has left terror,
nervousness, fear, headaches, and people seeing visions of the guerril-
las, of the army coming, who are going to persecute them, so they
have to run. For that, there is no medicine.

—Pedro Chom, health promoter in Santa María

T<small>HIS</small> <small>CHAPTER</small> will bring to center stage the enormous and, for some, crippling burden of the memories borne by the returnees and those who stayed in Guatemala. These memories, of course, were not neutral. The returnees pointed fingers and could name names. The revival and release of these memories on Guatemalan soil in itself were a threat to the army's control project. But those same memories represented a challenge to those holding them as well. The nature of their crippling force was a mystery to unravel. Many would need help to resolve the trauma.

In color and texture, these memories were gray and frozen, like rigid ice. As the returnees and those who stayed took on the challenge of reweaving their lives, these rigid gray strands caused distortion in the pattern. The memories could not be forgotten, and although gray had a place in the weave, it needed to be softened by enough healing to blend in with the rest.

When the refugees set foot on the land of Santa María Tzejá on May 18, 1994, an avalanche of memories was unleashed. While in Mexico they had told and retold their stories, which had reshaped their sense of the experience they had been through. But back in Santa María, they were in the very place from which they had fled in terror those eons/an instant ago. For a few, this was the land under which family members had been hastily and unceremoniously buried after they were massacred by the army on February 15, 1982.

For those who stayed in the village during the intervening years, the return also set adrenaline and memory in motion. Even though they had been on the land while the others had been away, the refugees' return ignited memories of the violence when the whole community, now freshly together, had been torn apart. Returning friends and family members triggered flashbacks that those who stayed had been warned not to talk about. With the returnees back and talking, the painful memories couldn't be avoided.

The talk spilling from these vivid memories represented a direct challenge to the army and to civil authorities. Army propaganda had had free rein in the Nation of Prisoners. In a total institution, the ruling ideology is the only one in town. All other thoughts are ruled subversive and can only be shared carefully out of the public eye by those brave enough to entertain them. Allowing fresh memories of the violence into public awareness would undermine the army line that the guerrillas had ultimately been responsible for the violence. With uncensored memories laid bare, the naked barbarity of the army atrocities could be aired in a way powerful enough to raise up defiance against the perpetrators.

To be sure, guerrilla leaders also had something to fear in the revival of the memories of the violence and the events leading up to the worst of it. They, too, on a far lesser scale, had killed civilians. Whatever their strategic objectives may have been at the time, their killings remained alive in memories they didn't control.

But just as surely as the release of memory at the return was a challenge to Guatemala, so too it was a challenge to the returnees themselves. Although they had lived free of the army, they hadn't escaped the ongoing psychological impact of the violence. A few had heard from medical personnel that some of the illnesses they suffered were rooted in the psychological impact of what they had been through, but they hadn't had help—or at least enough help—to unpack that pain. So they came back with much of that damage still causing what the medical world knows as stress/trauma-related illnesses.

Frozen Grief from Political Repression

Psychologists working as a team in four countries marred by the horrors of state terrorism—Chile, Argentina, El Salvador, and Guatemala—have struggled with the relationship between damage suffered by individuals within themselves and the social damage they suffer with the destruction of their communities. Their findings are directly applicable to Santa María Tzejá. The impact of state terrorism, as they see it, is more than psychological; it can more accurately be described as "psychosocial trauma" (Becker 1994, 95)—that is, the psychological effects of trauma when violent destruction is directed against a community.

Developing a conceptual framework, the four-country team began with the notion of "chronic fear." There is a paradox here, they note, given that fear is usually understood as a reaction to a specific threat (Becker 1994, 83). But in the context of constant threat from state terrorism, the fear becomes chronic, built into the internal psychological structures of the person.

When individuals have to deal on a regular basis with torture, exile, disappearance, and death, they lose the sense of boundary between reality and fantasy. Drawing here on another work by Chilean psychologists, the team calls attention to the damage that occurs when reality outstrips the wildest imaginings of one's worst fantasies.

In the face of unrelenting political repression and threat, social life is "traumatized and traumatizing" (Becker 1994, 83).

The team then moved on to a conceptual development for the term "trauma," noting that it was first named by Sigmund Freud and defined as "the notion of rupture and discontinuity in certain psychic processes." Bruno Bettelheim was the first to argue that trauma resulting from action of people consciously directed at other people is of a particular sort that can't be described in normal psychological language. It came to be called "extreme trauma" (Becker 1994, 84).

More recently, the team noted, Hans Keilson introduced the concept of "sequential traumatization" as a way of describing the reaction of individuals to ongoing political persecution. Keilson added the critical finding that the impact of the trauma continues after the terror has ended (Becker 1994, 85).

All of the team's observations encompass the experiences of the Guatemalan peasants who were driven from their homes in the scorched-earth violence of 1982. The initial horror of being dislocated and massacred and having their homes destroyed was augmented by the terror of hiding out from the army for months on their farmland. Even those who fled to Mexico carried the impact of the trauma with them, beyond the time of their firsthand experiences. For those who stayed, the continual repression of the army induced chronic fear.

A further concept is rooted in the experience of those who lost loved ones but because of extreme life circumstances were not able to express their grief through traditional customs. In this regard, the four-country team called attention to the work of I. Maldonado and E. Troya, who described this phenomenon as "frozen grief" (1988, in Becker 1994, 92). Because of external circumstances, the usual healing processes are blocked and the emotions of pain and loss are carried forward without relief. This circumstance certainly applied to those whose loved ones were killed in the massacres, but the rest who were driven from their homes and normal security had other reasons to grieve. Many were blocked in expressing it.

Finally, the team noted, all the concepts to this point applied primarily to individuals. What of the social phenomenon when whole communities were destroyed, when individuals were severed not only from their loved ones by death but from village life, from the entire community structure that had nourished them? To reach beyond the notion of the individual, the team turned to the thought of Ignacio Martín Baró, the Salvadoran social psychologist and priest who was one of six Jesuits murdered by the Salvadoran military on March 16, 1989. In his book, published posthumously in 1990, Martín Baró describes "psychosocial trauma"—that is, the interaction between the social as well as the psychological aspects of trauma caused by political repression (Becker 1994, 96).

The four-country team argued that there were different remedies, depending on how the analyst saw the circumstances of the trauma. To illustrate this point, the team described alternative approaches that might evolve after meeting a Guatemalan villager who survived the destruction of his village.

> When, for example, part of the political repression in Guatemala con-
> sisted in destroying whole villages, killing the population and distrib-
> uting it in other parts of the country, the objective was evidently to
> destroy indigenous communities. If years later we find ourselves with
> a survivor of these massacres, depending on the concept we use, we
> are going to perceive different dimensions of the problem. From the
> *extreme traumatization perspective,* we can understand the depressive
> framework that the survivor suffers; we would have an idea of the
> nightmares that were in her/his psyche, and we would try to develop
> an elaboration in which we recognize the damage inflicted on the
> person by the military and how the person could, one hoped, slowly
> realize the process of needed grief. From the *concept of psychosocial
> trauma,* we would understand that the central key of the trauma is
> the destruction of the indigenous community. We are going to under-
> stand the necessary reconceptualization of her/his cultural belonging
> and look for spaces where we can work in the reconstruction of her/
> his community belonging (Becker 1994, 97; emphasis added).

The authors argue that the two approaches are not mutually exclusive but that both should be taken into account and strategies developed for each.

Jacobo Timerman, in his book *Chile: Death in the South* (1987), uses a similar conceptual framework to describe what happened to a group of widows in the village of Calama. As noted in Chapter 2, Timerman calls attention to the symptoms psychiatrists see in victims of political repression: "depression, anxiety, insomnia, nightmares, diminution of intellectual powers, difficulties in sexual functioning, changes in family and emotional relationships, apathy, loss of memory" (29–30). In the women of Calama, there was, in addition, an "unresolved state of mourning"—the parallel to the "frozen grief" identified in the four-country study.

In analyzing what could be done to help the women heal, psychologists suggested a public and open ceremony at the cemetery. Children of the deceased would be there, and the women would tell their stories. The event would be collective in every way: "They told stories to each other, they all shared food prepared by the women themselves, and there were musicians to accompany the singing. They spent the day talking, remembering the past and revealing themselves, trying to come to terms with reality and with each other. Singing songs with familiar words was also good therapy" (Timerman 1987, 33). This experience was seen to help the women recover a sense of community, within which individual therapy could strengthen the person for fuller participation.

Chronic fear, extreme trauma, sequential traumatization, frozen grief, and psychosocial trauma are the terms, the concepts, the cumulative wisdom of experts who have struggled with the phenomena of political repression and state-sponsored terror. These analytical terms provide a framework for understanding the physical symptoms suffered by Guatemalans "for which there are no medicines" in the health promoter's formulation. These terms describe the ongoing damage inflicted on unarmed civilians whose communities were torn away from them and, in some cases, their loved ones murdered.

Dealing with Trauma and Frozen Grief

The traumatic reality experienced by the people of Santa María and other places throughout Guatemala in the early 1980s was far from abstract and analytical. It was sheer terror. People saw the smoke rise as their homes were burned and heard their animals being slaughtered. Some heard the gunfire as their loved ones were massacred. All had to survive for days, weeks, months on their land, away from the town center, and to cower in caves or ravines as army patrols made their sweeps or helicopters hovered overhead. Those who made their way to Mexico were terrified that they would be discovered on the way and shot. Those who were captured or gave themselves up feared the worst. Some of the men were tortured.

These experiences resulted in chronic fear, extreme trauma, sequential trauma, frozen grief, and psychosocial trauma. Yet these people carried on with their lives. The community of original settlers—all those still alive—is now back together, if not fully rewoven. Santa María thus becomes an important place to ask key questions: What are the ongoing effects of the trauma? And what is the community doing to deal with the villagers' traumatized memories and frozen grief?

During one of our church delegation's early visits, a doctor consulted directly with patients. (This was before the health promoters from the village had been trained. Once they had that training, doctors from our project stopped providing direct service.) The doctor was able to deal with the children's and the more obvious problems among the adults, but many adults complained of chronic internal pain, and without a laboratory, he couldn't make adequate diagnoses. He finally announced to those waiting that he could deal only with "new pains." What seems clear in hindsight is that many of the chronic problems were the result of the extreme trauma people had experienced in and following the violence.

In the quotation at the beginning of this chapter, one of the health promoters speaks of the nervousness, headaches, and nightmares people continued to experience. Reports of such symptoms have cropped up in a variety of conversations people from our delegations have had with residents of Santa María. The mention of a loved one who was killed in the violence can release tears that haven't stopped or been healed in the more than ten years since the violence. The open wounds were still much in evidence three years after the refugees returned.

How Santa María has been dealing with these wounds is worth noting. One part of the story grows out of the work of a person with a role unique to this village. He is Randall Shea, who, as noted in earlier chapters, wrote and helped Santa María's youth produce the play *The Past Is with Us*. A U.S. citizen, Shea gave up a lucrative business career to invest his life in Central America. After a time in Nicaragua, he went to southern Mexico, where he became a teacher to young refugees whose families were from Santa María. When they returned to Guatemala, he went with them and helped set up a middle school in the village.

Randall, known as "Rolando" in the village, had met a psychologist, James Crossen, who offered to come to Santa María as part of his sabbatical from a college in California. "Santiago," as he chose to be called in the village, had a gift for making people feel comfortable talking about their painful experiences, explaining to them that it would help them in healing their lives. There was no need to name the guilty, the ones who had caused them pain; simply talking about it in a safe place would give them relief, Crossen said. Given the opportunity, some fifty people came forward to talk about what they had been through. People felt relieved and were eager to participate in follow-up support groups that met once a week.

Pedro Canil spoke appreciatively of Santiago's work. He began by noting that the villagers had little understanding of the impact of the trauma before the experience of talking about it.

> Here in Guatemala this was the first time something like this happened, a massacre, a war, a terror so horrible. We never had ideas, experiences, as to how to heal these things. I certainly didn't know that holding all this in often causes damage to the person; I didn't know that. When we heard that many people were sick with nerves, that they couldn't sleep, that they couldn't feel comfortable psychologically there in Mexico . . . During the time we were there, when people went to health posts, the doctors said, you have these sicknesses because of what happened to you. What you are holding in is what is causing the damage. . . . So when we arrived here, thanks to God, Santiago came and he has as his profession having to do with all of these things, and since he understood all this, he began to work with the people here, especially the women. And they began to speak of this and to feel a little more peaceful regarding what happened (interview, November 1995).

Pedro's brother, Manuel, who lost many members of his family, had similar praise for Santiago:

> With the collaboration of Santiago Crossen, there are many people relieved a great deal, and we are thankful for that collaboration. Given the forces that hit us, there are many who need help to talk, so that little by little they can let go. For that, they need the idea of another person, like Santiago, who has studied a great deal of sickness and all that. We don't have the basis for helping a person, but with the help of Santiago . . . I am very thankful for that. There are many people, on the basis of that help, through his ideas, who have thought and reflected about things. That was a great help he gave us (interview, November 1995).

These men revealed the lack of understanding of psychological process that they had before the violence but also that there was no way they could have been prepared for the ferocity of the violence that hit them. They recognized the value of having someone available who was trained to deal with psychological problems of the magnitude they faced. But, more important, they were willing to place trust in this external helper, which could develop because of the relationship they had with Rolando during the three years when he was with them in Mexico.

So there were unique circumstances at work here. But the result indicates how important it is in a remote area of Guatemala—as it is in more developed parts of the world—to have someone trained in mental health to help people unpack the damaging pain of trauma. The question in a country like Guatemala, where there are very few trained mental health professionals, is how to provide for that need.

Thus, although there was frank admission in Santa María of the lack of understanding of mental health processes, there was an active recognition on the part of many I talked to of the importance of remembering the violence that had been inflicted on them. One man emphasized the critical nature of keeping memories alive, "so in the future someone who is governing can't do it again." Pedro Chom pointed to the importance for the children: "It is very important to have the memory and the history, that we speak and tell and express, so our children maintain the history as experience, so they understand the life, because they are the future. If we bury it, and forget all the memory and the history of our life, nothing will remain for the children. We will die, all of the older people, and the history will end there" (interview, November 1995).

There were also many people, perhaps a quarter of the population, according to estimates, who didn't want to hear about or discuss the past. "What happened, happened. Now I don't want to know anything about what happened," they said. But those who were very closed on the matter were a distinct minority. Many others, however, were nervous about where too much talk would lead. Most of those opposed to facing the past were people who had stayed, making this one more issue on the fault line between the two groups.

The issue of keeping the youth, the next generation, attuned to history was also addressed in Santa María in a unique way—through the play *The Past Is with Us*. The play provided a powerful bridge to the past. Young people who had gone through the violence as small babies but who had no personal memories of it were now able to appropriate those memories in a way that helped them experience them directly, as their testimony makes clear. After seeing a performance of the play in February 1996, the delegation from my church invited the young performers to describe their experiences and feelings in doing the play. One of them said:

> When one is presenting now it is like returning to the past, as if you were living in the moment in which these things happened. And actually, when one is acting, one feels as though one is living what happened. And at times this is a bit confusing, and makes you nervous. And in this moment my way of thinking is that what happened can't be buried but has to come to the light of day so that the whole world knows. For those who are guilty, we aren't so much interested in their being punished but that in some way they can feel in their hearts what they did.

Others spoke in a similar vein; doing the play made them nervous, they said, not because there were so many people in the audience but because they felt like they relived the events. They felt the sadness and pain their parents felt, and that they themselves experienced at some level, even though they were too young to remember.

One other issue remains to be dealt with in Santa María, the inescapable reality that the bodies of those massacred on February 15, 1982, were quickly buried without customary rites. The dignity due the remains and the survivors was denied by the circumstances. Grief was substantially frozen at that moment, blocked from its usual expression. A natural impulse is to want to exhume the remains and give them a dignified burial in the cemetery and, with that, to release the grief work that had been shut down by the unnatural conditions of the deaths.

But in Guatemala even such a profoundly human act as the exhumation and reburial of the remains of loved ones falls in the realm of controversy. At one level, any physical evidence of army massacres rekindles anger and memories of the larger events. Most immediately, it punctures the army's propaganda story and may make the guerrillas nervous as well—as Manuel Canil's testimony made clear:

> Regarding the possibility of exhumation, that's the basis for confirming what happened. For example, now the army says, "We are very respectful. Nothing happened here. What the people are saying is pure slander, that the army did it." So the exhumation is the basis for proving that, yes, there were violations of human rights. The guerrillas say, "We are very clean, it was the army that did it." Also, that will come out (interview, November 1995).

Once a decision was made to disinter the remains, another question pushed further into the controversial. Two options were possible, and both required the permission of local authorities. The first was to exhume and rebury the remains quietly, involving only local people and the local priest. Permission for this option would be easy to obtain, and the whole process would stay at a low profile. Even so, at the local level the process would revive memories and anger, with results that could not be entirely predicted.

The other option was to denounce publicly what happened, naming army units involved and leaders to the extent they were known. A wider cast of actors would be involved, including international forensic specialists, reporters, human rights workers, accompaniers, and so on. Permission for this kind of exhumation would be more difficult to get because the interests of key institutions, including the army, would be at stake. This path obviously would be more controversial at the local level as well, given the potential negative attention it would draw to the village. There would also be the possibility of death threats and harassment.

Families in Santa María whose loved ones were killed weighed their options carefully, burdened by their knowledge of what happened. As one of them said, "We can't deny what happened. We are witnesses to who killed them. They can't say we don't know." But they were not in a hurry, and they cared about the impact on the community. Their intent in the immediate years after the return was to wait until the final peace accords were signed.

In April 1997, after the peace accords were in place, the brothers Pedro and Manuel Canil began to explore the exact steps they would have to take to clear the way for the exhumation. Manuel went both to his village of origin and to that of his wife, killed in the massacre. He was told he couldn't get the papers in those places but would have to go to the judge in Cantabal, where the massacre took place. (The town of Cantabal is also the municipal center or capital of the area that includes Santa María.) At that point Manuel had plans to consult with human rights groups to determine what steps to take next.

Linked to the decision to exhume the remains was the possibility of raising a monument to the dead, telling when and under what circumstances they died—and at whose hands. Substantial monuments, with support from the U.S.-based Campaign for Peace and Life, had already been constructed in Rio Negro, in the nearby department of Alta Verapaz, and in Cuarto Pueblo, an Ixcán village not far from Santa María. Such monuments will preserve the memory of what happened for future generations and serve as reminders of the importance of vigilance, lest a similar thing happen in the future.

Santa María thus represented a microcosm of the issues related to the ongoing impact of the trauma caused by the scorched-earth violence and the resulting frozen grief. Its residents were back together, working to reweave their lives, but the effects of trauma distorted the pattern here, as elsewhere. Through a chance sequence of events— Randall Shea's living with them in Mexico, continuing back to Santa

María, inviting James Crossen to hold therapeutic conversations with the people, and then creating the play—a pattern for dealing with the painful memories was established. More, however, remained to be done, as the problem of what to do about the remains of those hastily buried made clear.

Recovering of Historical Memory Project

What about the other communities in Guatemala that suffered equal or worse violence? Where were they to get help? According to the peace accord, what is often referred to with a gloss of irony as the "Truth Commission" is supposed to give some attention to the heinous crimes committed against the civilian population. The very name of the commission, as noted in Chapter 3, reveals its intent to stop well short of the full truth: Commission on Clarification of Violations of Human Rights during the Armed Conflict in Guatemala.

Even though the accord was seen to be very weak and it contained no provision for naming the names of perpetrators or provision for legal redress, the very process of naming the massacres and other crimes and designating the institutions responsible would bring the facts to attention where other means might be found to deal with the pain. And the analysis that would accompany the report of the commission would provide a basis for public debate and, perhaps, some measure of social healing. After a series of delays following the December 1996 signing of the peace accords, the commission finally began its single year of work on July 31, 1997.

One group, the indigenous sector, represented by the alliance Defensoría Maya, took the work of the commission very seriously. Juan León, its leader, emphasized the role of the commission in gathering data:

> One role of the commission is to gather all the information regarding assassinations, disappearances, etc., as one means of clarifying what happened. Perhaps it won't name those responsible—that isn't provided for in the accord—but at least it can quantify things and name the victims. We, the Defensoría Maya, have been thinking about various types of follow-up after the commission finishes its work (interview, Guatemala City, June 1997).

Clearly, while wanting to make the commission as effective as possible, Léon saw its limitations. In a presentation in Washington in early June 1997, he described the depth of the problem faced by the indigenous population: "We face the challenge of how to cure the indigenous population that is so wounded by disappearances, murders, hate, and resentments festering within the community. How can we survive it? No one is dealing with the issues of mental health, but it is necessary" (author's notes, conference on Guatemala, Washington, D.C., June 1997).

One response to this need has been offered by the Roman Catholic church through its Recovering of Historical Memory (REMHI) project.

REMHI was originally conceived as an opportunity for people to give testimony, in as safe a setting as possible, about what happened to them in the violence. These testimonies would then be gathered, analyzed, and given to the "Truth Commission" to support its work. A central idea in the beginning, according to Edgar Gutierrez, the director of the project, was to try to understand the logic of political violence (interview, June 1997).

But those involved in the implementation of the project soon found that people needed space to open up, to talk about what they had gone through and suffered. They needed to be able to say that the army had come after them like dogs. They needed listening ears to explore their doubts about what sin they had committed to deserve what happened to them.

Gutierrez said that the REMHI project arrived late on the scene, in that fundamentalist churches had moved into the vacuum created in the aftermath of the violence. "What you suffered," the pastors said, "was punishment, the anger of God, so that you will correct your ways." People cried out, in the only space they found, but they didn't find relief.

The REMHI project was organized by the Roman Catholic church, starting with the bishops. The organizers had to talk with priests in the dioceses as well, to work through the fear that a truth-telling project like this raised. Questions came from priests who said that the army had set family against family, that, fifteen years after the violence, victims were living next door to perpetrators. How would it be possible, they asked, to create conditions that wouldn't cause people more pain? There would be need for vigilance, for follow-up. It wouldn't do just to come into someone's house, take information, and leave.

Conversations like that led the organizers to decide that the testimony takers would have to be local people from the communities where the interviews would be held. Moreover, they would need to be individuals highly respected for their moral strength. So the organizers decided to select interviewers very carefully and to form them into small groups for mutual support in what would be an emotionally draining and potentially politically dangerous undertaking.

Next, the REMHI organizers identified, recruited, and brought together a core of workers. They spoke the Mayan languages of the people they would be interviewing, because they were themselves from that ethnic group. Their training involved several facets. The first was to analyze the history of the violence in their own communities. In that context, the workers asked people to say what explanations they might have for the violence and thus to draw out interpretations that the people themselves would believe and "own." The second facet of the training involved discussing issues of mental health, including the nature of fear. The participants in the training were asked to "put [their] fears on the table and name them, and to see if they are so big they dominate you, or if they are ones you can dominate and plan to deal with." The third facet involved learning to do interviews, how to be with people in a way that let them get their feelings out. A related objective was to obtain information that would find its way into the report, given people's permission to allow that. In all, the training process took a year.

The next phase was to do the interviews, including necessary retraining as circumstances made that necessary. No one knew what to expect. Security precautions were thought through and shared regarding the possibility of interference from the army or infiltrators; conversations focused on how to protect cassettes that held testimonies and so on. Fortunately, the interviewers did not have unusually difficult problems.

Throughout the country, the interviewers took more than seven thousand testimonies, and by the time of Gutierrez's presentation in June 1997, more than five thousand of them had been processed. The testimonies were then analyzed by region in four categories: (1) sociopolitical and military effects, (2) psychological implications, (3) cultural impacts, and (4) legal issues. A fifth category under consideration at the time was the impact of the massacres on women.

Discussion was under way as well concerning follow-up in the communities. How could the analysis be shared with people in a way that would promote healing? Several issues needed to be thought through: mental health services, support for doing exhumations of the victims of massacres, providing resources to communities in the area of conflict resolution, and making available means through which people could recreate their histories with understanding of what happened. The hope was that the process would be an educational one—education for peace. The hope, as well, was that participants would gain insights and attitudes that would head off the possibility of the violence ever recurring (Edgar Gutierrez, workshop, Washington, D.C., June 1997).

The REMHI project was clearly an ambitious undertaking, and critical decisions remained to be worked out. One was the tone and content of the final report, due in March 1998. An early hope was to name the names of perpetrators of crimes against the population. But, as noted above, some lived next door to survivors or the families of victims, in which case naming the violators could lead to further violence. These issues had to be sorted out and the final report shaped around very complicated issues.

Should the report be issued on schedule, it would appear during the year of the "Truth Commission's" work. The two processes would then be joined, with an impact that no one can predict.

Conclusion

As each new group of refugees returned to Guatemala, an avalanche of memories was inevitably set in motion. Along with the joy of being back in their own country came flashbacks of the violence when they left, accompanied by terror-provoked adrenaline and the feelings they had in leaving. And their memories inevitably triggered memories in the people they touched on their return. The grief was unfrozen, if only for the short time of the return.

Whatever the intention of the returnees, this unleashing of memories created a challenge for the army and ruling authorities generally. It challenged the prevailing world view they were trying to maintain through the state propaganda apparatus. It unsettled the control mechanisms they used to maintain dominance. This returnee force, who had formed its attitudes and plans away from the army's control, was now back with its memories churning.

But if those memories were challenging the ruling authorities, they were also clearly disturbing to the returnees and to those who stayed. As the memories were renewed, so were the headaches, sleeplessness, and nightmares, the symptoms of unresolved trauma and frozen grief. How to bring healing to this gray pain, particularly when many people didn't realize the importance of talking about it, and fear levels were so high?

The experience of the people of Santa María Tzejá illustrates how important the mechanisms of healing can be. It was fortunate that outside professionals had earned the trust of the people and could help them release some of their pain. The mental health consultations have been praised by people who participated in them. Out of them the text for the play was created, which provided young people a platform from which to experience what their parents went through and what they themselves experienced before their memories were formed. But even in Santa María, the process of healing had just begun. Many were still too fearful to participate.

In the rest of the country, the REMHI project took on the burden of training testimony takers, who began the process of providing an outlet for the trauma that continued to hurt so intensely.

What was clear from all this was that people who were hurt internally by the violence needed a safe place where they could talk about what they went through and how it affected them. Beyond that safe space, however, they needed the assurance that what they said would not be used against them. And they needed follow-up from trained mental health workers, support for exhumations, training in conflict resolution, and assistance in healing and rebuilding their communities. REMHI leaders were aware of these needs and committed to helping to meet them. But the demands were enormous.

Outsiders, for the most part, can do little as counselors because of trust issues. But outsiders can provide a measure of security for communities within which the healing process can more productively go on. Internationals who are in a village during this process are able to give returnees the confidence that there is less likelihood of retribution or attack from the authorities, given outsiders are there as witnesses. In that way we who spend time in a community help provide the framework within which people feel the space and comfort to talk about what happened.

Now that the "firm and lasting" peace accords have been signed and the provisions are being contested by opposing interests, informed observers will be watching to see if "peace" will be only the absence or the lessening of overt conflict while the structural inequities that led to the war in the first place continue. Or will "peace" lead to holistic healing? If the former, grief will remain a frozen, rigid gray, a profound distortion of life in the Guatemalan social fabric. If the latter, healing and the rebuilding of community will soften the gray, which will then take its place in the spectrum of colors as the reweaving continues.

A critical factor in how the trauma and grief are resolved in the years ahead will be the role of the army. In a country still owned and governed by a few, will the military be realistically limited to guarding the borders and the police effectively trained and equipped to maintain a rule of law that makes real the progressive nature of the constitution? The peace accords themselves include some provisions that lead toward a positive answer to that question. But the accords are vaguely enough worded to allow slippage. The role and likely future of the army are the themes of the next chapter.

CHAPTER EIGHT

Tearing Still?

The Army in Peacetime

> *El Periodico* published information about the strategies of the
> army to maintain its position of power in the country, based
> on information gathered from army documents leaked to it. The
> primary document is entitled "Operation Plan—Transition to
> Peace '97." What is described in the plan amounts to counter-
> insurgency for peacetime.
>
> — Quoted in Long, *Situation Report 50*

WITH THE signing of the Accord for a Firm and Lasting
Peace in December 1996, the social and political atmosphere in Guatemala changed dramatically. People felt freer to
speak openly about what had happened to them. The newspapers
and airwaves were full of news about steps taken to fulfill one or the
other provision of the peace accords. The army's public information
office was aggressive in calling attention to the measures it was taking
to reduce its forces, in line with the timeframes set down in the Accord on the Role of the Army in a Democratic Society. In fact, the
army was in the process of recreating itself, including ferreting out
some of its most nefarious corrupt and criminal elements. Evidence
of its astounding new image was the joint presence of the guerrilla
commanders with the High Command of the Army at the Army Day
parade on June 30, 1997 (*Prense Libre*, July 4, 1997).

Yet all the shared platforms and strained embraces of former enemies could not wipe away the horrible reality of the past two decades—50,000 disappeared, 150,000 killed, 250,000 forced into exile, 1,000,000 displaced, and 45,000 widowed (Jeffrey 1996).[1] Nor
could embraces erase the history of a military institution that was

formed to protect the interests of international corporations and that served the interests of wealth and privilege. What that army had been during much of its existence was better glimpsed from the vantage of less than twelve years earlier.

My first impression, upon visiting the Ixcán region in December 1985, was the absolute brilliance of the army's strategy for controlling the population. The combination of dispersed army posts, tightly laid-out model villages, coordinating committees controlling the flow of resources to the area, and civil patrols creating a bondage system for all men added up to efficient domination of a terrified population. Having gained control, the army was already positioning itself with the civilian government that would soon take power.

Brilliant, yes, but barbaric. Attila the Hun could have learned from the masterminds of the scorched-earth campaign and its aftermath. One such self-identified mastermind was General Hector Gramajo, Minister of Defense under Guatemala's postdictatorship civilian president, Vinicio Cerezo, who took office in January 1986. Gramajo described his "more humanitarian" approach to managing the poor majority of the populace as providing "development for 70 percent of the population while we kill 30 percent. Before, the strategy was to kill 100 percent" (Schirmer 1991, 11). Even though the 30 percent figure was symbolic, the intent was clearly to indicate that the army would kill as many as necessary to maintain iron-fisted control. It would, that is, not hesitate to continue tearing at the fabric of Guatemalan society.

Of all the challenges the refugees faced on their return, this was perhaps the most daunting of all: how to forge the necessary political space, free of army interference, to pursue their hope for peaceful development and better lives for their children. This chapter analyzes how the villagers of Santa María faced this challenge.

The period just after the signing of the accords was a difficult one for the return movement. In the first six months of 1997, there were no returns at all, although there was social movement and political organizing. Reconciliation was in the air—to an extent at least. But countercurrents were blowing as well. Notably absent from the list of positive changes was the economic situation. Daily subsistence levels for the majority of the population, including the returnees, were not increasing; rather, the struggle for basic necessities was becoming more difficult. As noted in Chapter 3, desperate campesinos were demanding land and moving onto privately held plantations, claiming the land had been taken from them. A surge in violent crime suggested to some that shadowy forces were creating instability to stir a demand for the army to bring order.

And, as always, the army was a lurking presence. In the "post-peace-signing" era, the returnees and their allies had to assess the challenges they faced with the newly reimaged army. Taken as a whole, the activities of the army, at that point, revealed a complex pattern of contradictions. Its public persona was fully in step with the peace process. At the same time, its functions included working with the police to control crime and to drive off campesinos who were occupying plantations. In rural areas, there were credible reports that the army was mixing promises and threats to maintain control. And the newspapers carried a steady stream of reports of army figures who had committed crimes. As an institution, the army seemed to be biding its time, testing the limits of its power, and ready to resume as much of its prepeace role as the countervailing forces would allow.

Strategy, Resources, and the Will to Kill Prior to Signing the Peace Accords

While General Gramajo was at Harvard in 1990 burnishing his image with a graduate degree, Jennifer Schirmer, an expert on the Guatemalan army, was able to interview him at length. Her goal was to gain a perspective on the army from one of the shapers of its worldview, and Gramajo was forthcoming. His description was of an army that defined itself as constitutional and as a defender of the state. It understood itself as the continuity of the state and as co-governing with whatever party was in elected power at the moment. As co-governor, its particular responsibility was national security, over which it had exclusive control—while it left foreign affairs and human rights issues to the civilian government.

In his formulation, General Gramajo was in the historic mainstream of Latin American military thinking. In the formation of

Central and South American nation-states, armies had played a key role. They had been the only truly national institutions and had served as the guardians of the nations' primary values—as they defined them. Their central concept was the *patria*, a nationalistic alternative to the *fatherland*, which was to be protected at all costs. They were, as Gramajo argued, the continuity of the state, "above" the government currently in power. Should politicians try to sacrifice the long-term interests of the state for short-term gain, the army logically would feel obliged to intervene (Loveman 1998, chap. 2).

The Guatemalan army's framework for analyzing and responding to social unrest, as Gramajo explained it, was particularly revealing. The army had identified four levels of social conditions, each more dangerous and more in need of control than the previous. The first was the level of *"antagonisms,"* negative social problems, such as illiteracy or low wages—the whole range of social conditions that might generate unrest and opposition to the government. The second was the level of *"vulnerability,"* seen by the army as the point at which citizens who experienced antagonisms were vulnerable to the manipulation of outside agitators. The third was the level of *"pressure,"* at which point citizens focused their struggle against the state without realizing the significance of what they were doing. The fourth was the level of *"threat,"* when resisters took up arms and the army had to use violence against rebels, who were invariably supplied by an outside power such as Cuba (Schirmer, talk, Harvard University, 1995).

In the army's view, all antagonisms had the tendency to escalate into pressure, so the way to respond was to cut off dissent at the lowest levels. General Gramajo was at pains to tell Schirmer that people were free to complain, as long as they didn't go outside the law, which in a country as repressive as Guatemala was tantamount to saying their voices would not be heard. Even nonviolent protest in the form of marching on the street interfered with motorists' rights to the street, so the protesters were outside the law and had to be prosecuted. Dissent, in other words, could not be allowed because it always tended toward the next, more dangerous level. When it reached the "threat" level, as stated in the "develop 70 percent, kill 30 percent" formula, no level of killing was beyond the pale.

That was the army's strategy, to cut off even the slightest whiff of resistance as early as possible, so it would not escalate. But the army had more than a strategy. It had resources—official budgetary support from the state, unofficial state support, media outlets, its own official businesses, and unknown off-the-books profits that flowed to powerful forces that were themselves the "law." One source reported that, although the army had a line of 8 percent of the national budget, in reality, because of transfers to the military from other ministries, it spent 46 percent. Further, the army had its own social security institute, which allowed it to invest inside and outside the country. Plus, it had legal businesses—its own bank and television station—as well as illegal businesses. Its tentacles were everywhere (interview, Juan Quiñones, Center for Human Rights Legal Action, November 1995).

Enter the returning refugees, whose thinking, from the army's perspective, had been "manipulated" by uncontrolled exposure to ideas about human rights and democracy. The army knew the refugees had interacted with the guerrillas. It knew the returnees had learned about the Guatemalan constitution and U.N. human rights documents. The army knew, as well, that the returnees had conducted an analysis of the army's role in the violence of 1982. The returnees, in short, were loose cannons on the Guatemalan deck. In their time away from the army's control, they had become outside agitators, sure to exploit vulnerabilities (level two on the scale above) among the poor majority, who would then try to exert national and international pressure (level three) and eventually threat (level four).

Yet, even at that time, the Guatemalan army realized it was living in a new national and international climate. As the likelihood of a final settlement of the war increased, the army faced a new challenge to its function. Key officers committed to working within the constitutional framework took it on themselves to rework their own institution. As one of them told Schirmer, "We have to clean our own house, or there won't be any house to clean. We won't wait for the civilians to give us a list of what must be changed. We must redefine our own role." Schirmer said that, from her perspective, the army was grappling then with how to conduct a society by way of an army (interview, December 1995).

Even before the signing of the final peace agreements, the army agreed to the elimination in all communities of its key representatives, called military commissioners, who had served not only as the army's eyes and ears but as its recruiters of new soldiers. In addition, the civil patrols were phased out. Both functions were ended, however, at a time and in a way that gave the army control of the process (Jeffrey 1996, 8).

When President Arzú first came to power, the army permitted a few of its top officers to be sacked, those most notoriously involved in corruption or high-profile human rights violations. Later, just before the signing of the accord on the army, others were cashiered who were involved in a massive smuggling ring under the leadership of a customs official, Alfredo Moreno Molina. The month before the signing, another ninety-one officers accepted early retirement, though an army spokesperson denied there was any purging of officers involved in corruption and abuse (Schirmer, phone conversation, September 1996).

When the Accord on the Strengthening of Civilian Authority and the Role of the Army in a Democratic Society was signed in September 1996, the equation changed somewhat. The agreement called for the army to cease being a force that occupied the country for security purposes. It was barred from diverting civil patrols to being transformed into development committees—or anything else. Its only function would be to defend the borders of the country, except in the case of clearly delineated emergencies. That was what was on paper (NISGUA 1996, 1). How it would be interpreted was another matter.

Santa María's Challenge to the Army and Its Attempts to Intimidate in Return

In early May 1994, the newcomers who had occupied lands vacated by the refugees left, having been paid by a government agency for the improvements they made on the land. Shortly before, the army had decommissioned the civil patrol and collected army-owned weapons. Then, on May 13, the largest group of refugees returned—all original settlers—to take up life again in the village, followed a few days later by a smaller group that came from a different state in Mexico. A miracle of sorts had taken place, in that nearly the entire original population of Santa María, plus the children born to them during the exile period, minus those massacred or who died of other causes, were now back together.

Santa María was unique in that roughly half the original settlers returned in organized groups from Mexico, and the other half were original settlers who stayed. Because the two groups were nearly balanced in size, one not overwhelming the other, the village presented a good challenge to the army's plan to keep the two subpopulations divided. The army's goal was apparent in the strained relationships in the early days after the return: those who stayed maintained high levels of suspicion and refused to have anything to do with the returnee organizations.

Unfortunately, from the army's perspective, its expectations were not met. The returnees had no horns or tails and were not radical rabble-rousers. They worked hard and contributed to the community. Even their talk about human rights was compelling for those who stayed, when they could get past their fears enough to listen. Further, although there were still tensions, members of both groups came to feel that the community had been able to reweave its torn life.

For the army, then, the news out of Santa María was bad. The village had become, as Padre Beto said, "lost territory" to the army. Rather than staying divided, it stood a chance of becoming a launching pad for human rights education in the area and a model for the country. As such, it posed a significant challenge to army control (interview, Padre Beto, November 1995).

The army had tried hard to make sure Santa María stayed divided. One of the returnees described what he heard from those who stayed:

> [The army] prepared the people in its way of thinking, . . . and [the soldiers] continue creating fear, saying the war will come again soon. They say the returnees are going to last only three years, and "one by one we are going to get you if you take the side of the returnees. You should form a group apart from the returnees, and we will maintain direct communication with you, so you will come out OK in the hour of the problem. Those who don't identify with us, who don't maintain communication with us, will be in trouble. . . . In whatever

moment we will deliver arms to you, and rise up again." So, this doesn't help with reintegration, or promote unity. It is, rather, a kind of "help" that causes deep division and stimulates and provokes problems. So this is what the army is doing. It doesn't want to promote unity, integration, and peace (interview, November 1995).

Another man noted how the army linked the returnees with the guerrillas: "They say things like that to terrify the people, in order to continue causing division between the returnees and those who stayed. This is nothing more than to cause division. Through this division, they can control. In contrast, when the people organize themselves in just one group, it isn't so easy for the army to do what it wants" (interview, November 1995).

In May 1994, right after arriving back in Santa María, a returnee described the approach the returnees would take to the army. They wouldn't provoke it, he said, but they would not back down if the army tried to dominate and impose its will. One important factor that would help the returnees would be the ongoing presence of international accompaniers, who would get the word out if the army moved on the returnees. "We want witnesses," another man told me.

A good example of the stance the returnees took in practice is provided in their response to a threat by a man who stayed in the community during the exile. He had been using common land that belonged to the cooperative to grow and harvest crops for his own profit. Although that was against the rules, the rules hadn't been enforced on that point. When the returnees raised the issue and worked through the elected improvement committee to enforce the rule, the man threatened members of the committee, saying that if they kept on pushing him off the common land, a fate like the massacre at Xamán would befall Santa María (interview, November 1995).

On the face of it, this was a very serious threat. Improvement committee members weren't sure if the man was a frustrated loner or if perhaps he was being put up to the threat by others. The leaders of the village determined to find out, and if the trail led to the army, they would denounce its role in the matter before the world. As part of the investigative process, the leadership sent a delegation to the regional judge to establish a record on the issue, a legal framework, should further evidence come to light. Nothing further has surfaced on the matter, but the vigorous response of the community illustrates its determination not to be intimidated, even to the level of possible army involvement.

But if there was the sense that Santa María was lost territory to the army, the military institution wasn't going to stand by passively either. In October and November 1995, the army asserted its presence in three escalating events. The first occurred on October 6, when a delegation of ambassadors was scheduled to visit Santa María to see this model community of relatively successful reintegration. The army had insisted it would need to provide protection for the ambassadors. But the ambassadors never came, because of the massacre in Xamán the day before. All the helicopters that might have been used to carry the ambassadors to Santa María were in use for this terrible event. But, although the ambassadors were not able to come, an army contingent came anyway. The presence of seventy soldiers, just as the people of Santa María were hearing about the massacre in Xamán over the radio, was extremely unsettling.

Then, in early November, a company of five hundred soldiers passed through the village, with the advisory that this was simply a changeover of companies out in the field. Whatever the pretext, the sight of five hundred soldiers in the village was enough to cause high anxiety.

Two weeks later, a group of about 150 soldiers in battle gear, their faces blackened with greasepaint, came to the village one afternoon and stayed for the night in the center. All but one were in full uniform. The exception wore a black T-shirt, emblazoned with a helmeted skull clutching a dagger in its mouth. The words on the shirt said, in English, "Born to Kill." Although people in the village couldn't translate the words, the visual was frightening in itself.

The next day, the soldiers left the center of the village early but were reported as having visited the cornfields of at least two men. When they approached the men, the soldiers said no one had to worry about them, that they were human beings and were there to help the people. This was said by soldiers in battle gear against a backdrop of memories of burnings and massacres by this same army. (The author was in the village during this third visit by the army.)

A Guatemalan Presbyterian minister spoke about the impact of the presence of the army: "If the people see soldiers, this is a message, a strong one, for the people. The soldiers' great power is a power of presence." By simply passing through, the army was imposing its power on the people. The message reverberated through in the flashbacks and nightmares of the residents.

Fortunately, the people of Santa María reacted calmly, at least overtly. They knew the army had the right to pass through national territory and to provoke it during such an activity could lead to a tragedy like the one in Xamán, where people in the village had confronted soldiers on patrol. In that highly charged emotional atmosphere, the soldiers had opened fire. The people of Santa María avoided a similar tragedy by not responding to the soldiers.

Santa María illustrated in a powerful way the challenge returnees posed to the army. The village illustrated, as well, the way the army had of biding its time, establishing its presence, and working in the surrounding area to ensure there were "no more Santa María Tzejás." The overarching message the army sent from Xamán was that it would stop at nothing to keep its power intact.

The Unfolding "Role of the Army in a Democratic Society"

Speaking in Washington in June 1997, Frank LaRue, an exiled Guatemalan labor lawyer and founder of the Guatemala-based Center for Human Rights Legal Action (he returned to live in Guatemala in July 1997), stated flatly that the power of the Guatemalan army had not diminished since the signing of the peace accords. He argued that President Arzú had the same relationship to the army as previous governments. Worse, he was using the military to combat common crime on the streets. And, within the president's military guard, Arzú maintained a squadron to capture kidnappers, using illegal methods. Arzú's presidency, LaRue argued, was still weak and he needed to rely on the army to maintain himself.

Guatemala's ombudsman for human rights, Jorge García Laguardia, agreed with LaRue, saying that the army had unlawfully retained power in Guatemala because of the weakness of the state. Laguardia continued:

> That is certain because there has been a conservative conspiracy over the last forty years keyed to weakening the institutions of the state, to disparage politicians and public services. I think they have been successful, because the state is almost nonexistent, unseen anywhere except in urban areas and the capital. That has created a power vacuum that has been filled by delinquency and disorder. In the face of that disorder there are just two institutions with a national presence throughout the country, the army and the Catholic church. In any case, it is clear that it is the army that gives the orders (Interiano 1996).

And although spokespeople have maintained that the army is paying close attention to following through on the letter of the peace accords, many of the army's actions have conveyed an in-your-face denial of the spirit of the accords or, worse, open defiance of them. In January 1997, the military set up checkpoints in several rural areas and even on the Interamerican Highway (Cerigua 1997b). In February, the army began a new training session for the notorious Kaibil counterinsurgency force, a crack battalion involved in some of the worst abuses of the war. The director of the training school said that he saw little need to change anything, except that the word "counterinsurgency" would be dropped from its mission statement, "because there no longer was an insurgency" (Guatemala Human Rights Commission/USA 1997, 4). In February as well, the government announced that ex-soldiers were eligible to serve in the new national police force (Cerigua 1997c). In April, the troops were sent out on the street to support civil police in controlling crime (Cerigua 1997e).

In June 1997, Defensoría Maya issued a bulletin denouncing military activity in which soldiers, masquerading as a new guerrilla group, robbed, assaulted, and intimidated people in the provincial department of El Quiché. The group, charged the Maya organization, was trying to destabilize the area through the use of intimidation and terror, in order to derail the rule of law. Conditions were such, according to Defensoría Maya, that people with a militarized consciousness were thinking about recreating the civil patrols. Others were considering inviting the army to impose order. The army, said the group, was entering a range of communities, saying that the army was the only force that would meet the needs of the people and that they should not get involved with human rights groups or indigenous groups. The bulletin named places and dates where the army entered to intimidate the people. Summarizing the charges, Defensoría Maya said that the army

> continues violating, in a systematic way, the Global Accord on Human Rights and the Accord on the Identity and Rights of Indigenous Peoples. For the Maya people, the continuing presence of the army in our communities has limited the revaluing and recomposition of our communities. [Under these conditions,] we can't reconstitute our social fabric, nor recreate our political, economic, social, and cultural system (Defensoría Maya 1997).

These were serious charges, made on the basis of testimony received by a widely recognized indigenous organization. Defensoría Maya made the specific case, with dates and places, that the army continued to tear at the social fabric, thereby inhibiting the reweaving the people desperately wanted to pursue. But to these destructive actions could be added the equally serious charge that the army itself was deeply implicated in criminal activity. This had been generally known for years, but then, with the military in a position to want to clear its reputation, military arrests of active and retired personnel provided ongoing evidence of military involvement in crime.

A researcher on military affairs for a Washington-based agency has noted that she anticipates that the army will continue to justify having a major role in Guatemalan internal affairs. First, although by the accord dealing with the army, the military will be limited to defending the country's borders, the army will get around that limitation by defining a number of crimes as border-related. Illegal drugs will have come in over the borders, justifying work throughout the country to stop the traffickers. The same would be true of illegally entered cars and other forms of contraband. She noted that the defense ministers of Central America had staked out that role for their militaries. Second, the army could involve itself in development activities, including, as noted in Chapter 4, road building. Related activities might include responding to disaster relief and helping with vaccination campaigns—good image-building activities. Third, in a more indirect role, ex-military people could serve in the new national police. Many observers, Guatemalan and foreign, thought that was barred by the peace accord dealing with the military, but a close reading showed that not to be the case. Fourth, according to provisions in the peace accord, the army is allowed to cooperate in activities with other agencies. All this indicates a substantial, and potentially very powerful, role for the military in the post-peace-signing years (interview, Rachel Garst, June 1997).

In March 1997, an unnamed military source was cited in the daily newspaper *El Periodico* as saying that "hard-liners" in the army "are behind much of the organized crime wave that continues to plague the country." They arm and control many of Guatemala's criminal gangs, the source claimed. They seek to create such a level of instability that the army will be called in to restore order, thus increasing the army's power (Cerigua 1997a, 4).

In June, the minister of defense, General Julio Balconi, reported that twelve army officers had been sacked for their involvement in drug trafficking and that others were being investigated. He was at pains to point out that the army was being open about rooting out those in its ranks "at the margin of the law" and that the army was in the process of restructuring itself. But the regular appearance of such articles in the press was an indication of the depth of military involvement in crime, that the supposed guarantors of law and order were themselves its violators (Hernandez 1997).

Then, in late July 1997, President Arzú ordered the reopening of several military bases that had been closed, in response to the "struggle against violence" in rural areas. The unidentified author of the article reporting this news went on to condemn the action: "Using the army to fight violence, whether in cities or in the countryside, flies in the face of the spirit and letter of the peace accords, which call for a constitutional redefinition of the role of the army to include only defense of national borders" (Guatemala News and Information Bureau 1997b, 3).

The sum total of this information is that the army did not change in any profound way from what it was before the signing of the Accord for a Firm and Lasting Peace. Well-placed observers judged that the army retained the real power in Guatemala. Documented activities provided evidence of its continued harassment of rural communities and its significant involvement in organized crime. The army itself has identified several roles it can play within the letter, if not the spirit, of the peace accords that will allow it to maintain its activity throughout the country. An unnamed internal source stated that the army engaged in destabilizing criminal activity to stimulate the population to demand the use of the army to restore order. This unproved charge may have been the mischief of a disaffected officer. But the fact was that the president had indeed called out the army to restore order in the streets and was reopening bases in the countryside.

Conclusion

Guatemala, in the period just after the signing of the peace accords, was in a state of transition from thirty-six years of armed conflict—to what? No one was quite sure. The clearest indication was, as reported in Chapter 3, a transition, already well under way, to the country's becoming a more active player in the global economy. Arzú's unswerving policy of privatization and support for big business in the private sector provided the evidence.

One key variable in the transition was the role the army would take in the midterm future. Years of negotiation between the URNG and the government/army had yielded an accord with the army that had sent waves of hope through the country. Cutting the army's size and budget by one-third and limiting its mission to defending the country's borders were seen as good starting places. And the accord, "Strengthening of Civilian Authority and the Role of the Army in a Democratic Society," was judged to be important in both its major categories: civil and military.

Early indications were encouraging. There was substantial activity among the several civic sectors, particularly among the indigenous, women, and campesino sectors, including resurgences in organizing in labor and other sectors. And the army, as reported above, was careful to make the public aware that it was intent on fulfilling the accord.

On the one hand, for the returned refugees, and for those who waited in Mexico hoping to return, this was not an encouraging period. The return process had stalled. Divisions within the return population were polarizing some of the communities. And the struggle for adequate land continued. Many return communities, on the other hand, were working things out with those who stayed. But the economy wasn't working for them, either.

Given the poverty, the volatility of many rural communities, and the relative vacuum of state power in the countryside, as noted by the ombudsman for human rights, the behavior of the army—apart from its public presentation in the city—became a critical indicator for the future. In this respect, the prognosis was not encouraging. The army's recent history, prior to the signing of the accords and prior to the return of the refugees, had been one of total and brutal control.

Things do not change from the night to the morning, as they say in Guatemala. Another saying posits the obvious, that between what is said and what is done, there is a great distance. If the 1980s were the night, the morning of the signing of the accords in the mid-1990s was not very removed in time. And, clearly, there was a great distance between what had been said about compliance in the city and what had been done in rural areas. It seemed clear as well, from what Jennifer Schirmer learned from her interviews, that the army had been planning for some time to stay ahead of the change curve, to participate in the peace accords while still maintaining as much power as possible.

Yet, in the face of all the accumulated reasons for caution and concern, there were some sources of hope. One was the accord itself, which cut the size and budget of the military and limited the scope of its mission. Held to those provisions, the army would lose a significant measure of power. The document existed in a framework of international verification for current and future activism and enforcement.

Another source of hope was the presence and pressure of the refugee return movement. Although it had lost momentum as a result of all the obstacles it faced and its own internal divisions by the time of the signing of the peace accords, it still had an impact. If Santa María Tzejá was "lost territory" to the control project of the army, there were other "lost" communities as well. They would serve as thorns in the side of the ruling authorities and as models for others, with the message that if they came together, if they reweaved their lives, there would be hope for development and a better future. Such communities wanted and needed solidarity support that included both presence and resources.

The latter point leads to a third reason for hope but one that is laced with contradictions: international pressure. At the level of nations, the international "community" pressured for an end to the war, a measure of support for human rights, and a recognizable reduction in the size of the Guatemalan army, which had a reputation for serious human rights violations. And the international donor community pledged almost $2 billion (70 percent of it in loans) for the rebuilding of the country. These are all potentially positive signs. But there is no reason to turn away in careless optimism. There is, in reality, little reason to believe the Arzú government, with its strong commitment to big business and the private economy, will direct much of the new resources to meeting the needs of the broad majority of the population.

That reality signals the importance of the other form of international pressure, from a variety of sources within the solidarity movement, including nongovernment organizations and church and secular groups. Support and pressure are needed in a great variety of settings. The final chapter suggests some strategies for involvement.

CHAPTER NINE

Weaving the Future
What Needs to Be Done and How to Get Involved

*[The United States'] role in toppling the reform movement in 1954
and supporting brutal authoritarian rule for three decades have
shaped political life in Guatemala and made it so difficult to establish a rule of law in the county.*

—Barry, "Guatemala: A Test for Democratization"

WHEN THE Guatemalan refugees crossed the border
from Mexico on January 20, 1993, during the first organized collective and voluntary return provided by the accords
signed on October 8 of the year before, emotions ran high. As more
than seventy buses passed into Guatemala, a roar went up from the
waiting crowd of officials and everyday folks who had gathered for
this momentous event. Rigoberta Menchú, Guatemala's newly selected Nobel laureate, was there to represent the indigenous majority
of the nation and to symbolize its welcome. Returnees and those in
the welcoming crowd alike all hoped this was a first step in the re-
uniting and healing of a people still suffering from the effects of a
violent civil war.

Yet the enthusiasm and joy of that moment soon gave way to division and rancor in Victoria, the return community to which these
refugees were wending their way. There would be factional infighting
in other communities as well, most notably in the Ixcán Grande
cooperatives, as described in Chapter 5. This chapter seeks to understand these setbacks in the context of the deeply polarized Guatemalan social landscape.

Yet, as important as those setbacks were, they constituted only one
dimension of the organized flow of refugees across the border that

took place in the years following the signing of the October 8, 1992, accords. Taken as a whole, the return movement had substantial impact throughout the country; the refugees did return to challenge Guatemala. And, although the setbacks received more press, particularly in Guatemala, there were important successes as well, as the case study material from Santa María Tzejá illustrates. This chapter assesses the impact of the return and includes recommendations for future returns to Guatemala and elsewhere.

Finally, this chapter turns to questions that directly involve all of us who become aware of the conditions in Guatemala: First, why become involved now, when the "Guatemalan problem" seems to be resolved as a result of the successful completion of the signing of the peace accords? Second, for those who see the need to continue in solidarity, what needs to be done, and how can they get involved?

Divisions, Successes, and Assessment

Although there had been delays leading up to that first return to Victoria, the returnees were filled with hope and determination. They had come back to challenge the Guatemalan army and state authorities to let them live and develop in peace. As they began to build their community, they found themselves courted by agencies and organizations with offers to help. International accompaniers were everywhere. This was the first big return, and the eyes of the world were watching.

Government agencies and the army had braced themselves for this event. The return represented the first of many that would potentially involve tens of thousands of people who had formed attitudes and plans away from the dominance of the Guatemalan army. No one could predict how disruptive the returnees might be. With that in mind, the authorities had tried to slip them back into the country by a short, direct road over the Mexican border, through a town called Ingenieros, so there would be little notice, but the refugees had insisted on the widely publicized route through the capital.

The return to Victoria appeared to pave the way for other successful returns later in the spring. But four years later, at the time of the signing of the peace accords, that first return community could hardly be described as a community at all. It was deeply divided, so riven, in fact, that there were two separate sets of schools and two town offices, serving the two main factions.

Across the Chixoy River and a little to the west, the Ixcán Grande population was equally divided by the time of the signing of the "firm and lasting peace" in December 1996. These two major refugee resettlement areas were thus in disarray. One could fairly ask, on the basis of these two major returns, whether the refugees had come back to challenge Guatemala or to quarrel among themselves. Among sources consulted for this book, there was frustration and disappointment that key areas of the return movement were so divided.

What had gone wrong? The whole story has not been uncovered. Researching and analyzing it would take another book. Certainly there were differences within the refugee community in Mexico regarding the nature and pace of development. There also was the residue of earlier disputes within the Ixcán Grande cooperatives that could be traced to the period before the violence. But equally important were the attitudes subgroups took toward the guerrillas' strategies for the postreturn period. Some, like the first board of directors of the Ixcán Grande and the board in Victoria, maintained strategic alliances with the guerrillas. Others were drawn to an alternative approach to development, led by members of the Permanent Commissions, the elected representatives of the refugee communities who had negotiated the conditions of the returns.

In the highly charged and oppressive political environment of rural Guatemala at the time of the returns, the return communities naturally came under pressure and were subject to exploitative manipulation by opposing forces. Neighbors were set against neighbor. Energy that should have been directed toward challenging the injustices of the system was often directed internally.

But although the disputes in Victoria and the Ixcán Grande cooperatives were important and drew widespread attention, they did not begin to constitute the whole story. Put in perspective, they were part of a movement that did challenge Guatemala on the issues discussed in this book. While acknowledging that the return movement had lost some of its force because of internal divisions, Cesar Díaz, direc-

tor of the development agency Alianza, pointed out that the returnees "ignited the life of this country, and continue to do so" (interview, June 1997).

Another well-placed observer, Dan Long, expanded on that point.
The returnees had made an impact, he said, first, because they
came back under a negotiated set of accords that gave them leverage with the government. Under the terms of those accords, the
returnees would get land—not necessarily (or, as it turned out,
even likely) the land they had left, but land nonetheless. That guarantee was not part of the later peace accord on the displaced and
uprooted, which applied to those who had been driven from their
homes, including refugees. But only the refugees who were covered
by the October 8, 1992 accords had a claim to land (interview,
June 1997).[1]

The second major reason the returnees made an impact was the
fact that they were highly organized. They were not as intimidated
by dominant authority as those who stayed. They knew their rights
and where to turn to demand them. And they had experience in
resorting to support structures and mediation when problems threatened to fly out of control. Although emotions were explosive in both
Victoria and the Ixcán Grande, as Long pointed out, there was relatively little violence. Mediators gained access and arranged cooling-
off periods.

The third reason the returnees made an impact lay in the fact that
international funds provided support. Beyond the initial provision of
food, tools, and roofing materials necessary to get the returnees resettled, aid was made available to the subregions where the returnees
located and thus benefited their neighbors as well. Long pointed to
one of what he said could be "hundreds of examples." A road had
been built to the community of Entre Rios which served fifteen other
villages along the way. Representatives of those villages then met with
the returnees to determine what other benefits their villages might be
able to get. Long noted, further, that issues of health and education
were on the table for rural communities because of the returns.

No one should be surprised that there are serious problems in a
country that has a long history of violence and oppression, Long

argued. But without the refugee returns, he said, there would be little awareness of the problems. The only news would have been vague reports of campesinos who were killed. Even when the returnees were arguing among themselves, they knew how to get their stories out to where the problems could be addressed.

In other words, the return movement had a major impact in spite of the serious divisions that were generated within some return communities. More positive evidence of the impact came from communities like Santa María, where the returnees reintegrated with those who stayed and reached out to surrounding communities to expand the social reweaving process. Such communities demonstrated that in many settings the authorities' efforts to keep people divided did not succeed.

In Santa María, the first year after the return in May 1994 was fraught with tension and issues between returnees and those who stayed. But careful preparation of the refugees in Mexico, maturity, patience, and effective leadership all around led to easing of the tensions and movement toward positive cooperation. The primary school and the new junior high were central to this process. Daily learning together led children and youth to forget who had grown up where. In an interview in June 1997 with three young people, recounted earlier, each said they could hardly remember the strains that had been evident between the two groups just after the return. Men and women worked together on common projects with no reference to whether they had been in Mexico or stayed in Guatemala. Only among the catechists was there a residue of sensitivity about their different approaches to the faith, which had roots in the subcultures of learning and fear.

And like Entre Rios, where the new road benefited fifteen neighboring communities, Santa María had an impact on its region and beyond. By August 1997, even the primary school enrolled students from two other communities, and the junior high had both day students and boarders from several other villages. Unlike other villages in the Ixcán region, all the teachers in Santa María were from and lived in the village itself. Their work was disciplined and thorough. The curriculum, as reported earlier, drew on the students' experiences but also incorporated recent history so the learners would come to understand the reasons for the country's poverty, repression, and violence.

Through performances of the play *The Past Is with Us*, the story of the violence in Santa María was made available to communities throughout Guatemala. Scenes from the play were filmed by a Canadian television crew and by the British Broadcasting Corporation. A video called *The Terror and the Truth* portrays scenes not only from the play but of the actors on tour, noting that in some remote villages people hadn't realized that the violence of the early 1980s had been so generalized and thought it had perhaps only happened to them or in their immediate areas. Scenes captured the villagers' deep emotion in seeing the young people of Santa María reenact what had also been these villagers' experiences. Commentators in the video reasoned that only through engaging the truth at such a profound emotional level would victims of the violence come to find healing. Through the theater tours and the filming of the play, then, the emphasis on human rights and emotional healing taking place in Santa María was extended throughout Guatemala and the world beyond.

The experiences of the villagers of Santa María Tzejá suggest a number of lessons that may be useful for returnees elsewhere. The recommendations that follow may be particularly appropriate in cases in which the experiences of separated residents contrast sharply and when a number of years have passed between taking refuge and returning. These suggestions are for those involved directly in refugee returns.

Recommendations for Future Returns

First, in the period before the return, discuss in detail with the refugees the experiences and subcultures of those who did not flee. Returnees to Santa María described the workshops and daily meetings they had just prior to the return. A key topic was what life had been like for those who stayed, including how those in Guatemala would be likely to view the returnees. Fortified with that knowledge, the returnees were more prepared to see past the effects army propaganda had on the minds of those who stayed. And they were prepared to be more patient with those people who were subject to constant military domination through the years of separation. Because of that preparation and the experience of working things through with those who stayed, the two groups were more able to learn from each other.

Second, train members of return groups to be able to identify and work through the ideological differences that exist within their groups. This may be particularly important in settings where the whole population consists of returnees. Ironically, perhaps, the people who returned to Victoria and the Ixcán Grande did not have the immediate foil of having to deal with a population whose experience contrasted so dramatically with their own. Other factors were at work, as noted above. But, based on the experiences of these all-returnee communities, internal conflicts should be anticipated and returnees prepared even more strongly so that they can turn to mediation as soon as necessary. One informant in Santa María mentioned that immediately following the return he looked wistfully at the all-returnee groups, thinking it would be better if they didn't have to work through problems with those who stayed. By the time he shared that thought, however, he felt fortunate to have been forced to resolve issues with those who had extensive experience dealing with Guatemalan realities and noted that Santa María was coming together, while the residents of other villagers were at odds.

Third, anticipate with both the returnee group and the receiving group that there will be many sources of tension growing out of their vastly different experiences during the time of separation. The author's experience over the years with the original settlers in Santa María who stayed was that they had high expectations for welcoming back their friends and relatives, without a corresponding sense of how different their experiences had been. So they were surprised and caught off guard and even had the sense of being dominated and put down for a time by the returnees. With that in mind, it is useful to review the experience of a community like Santa María to learn about the great range of issues that are likely to surface. These issues are discussed at length in Chapter 4. One of the key issues was that those who lived under the authority of the army were oriented to obey authority, not only in relation to the military itself but in such areas as education. Those who stayed had much greater difficulty imagining their children could learn as well from educators drawn from the community population as they could from state-provided and credentialed teachers. Experience over time convinced those who stayed that they were wrong on that point.

Fourth, prepare the refugees carefully regarding the complexities of development that will confront them once they return. Evidence drawn from interviews in Santa María suggests that neither group was adequately prepared for the myriad development opportunities to which they would have to respond. Central to this recommendation is a conception of integral development in which the process starts with the visions, plans, and initiatives of people at the most local levels. This does not preclude development planning at other nongovernment and government levels, but it does suggest that agencies need to give highest priority to working to empower people in a culturally sensitive way at the most local levels. Another implication is that progressive education should be offered to enable people to understand global economic forces and how they affect the local economy. In Santa María, this concern focused on issues having to do with the markets for the villagers' agricultural products, oil exploration, timber exploitation, and maquila manufacturing.

Fifth, offer refugees human rights education from the beginning of their refugee experience and, where possible, in the communities that will receive them. Informants in Santa María reported that there was a rush of human rights workshops within the year before the return but that was eleven years after their arrival in Mexico. If refugees are to be understood to be full human beings, they deserve to know their rights from the beginning.

Sixth, address issues of mental and emotional healing as soon as resources are available, well before the refugees return. This is critically important when a population is as highly traumatized as the Guatemalan refugees were. If the matter is left until after the return, it becomes even more complex, because some of the perpetrators may live close at hand. Training mature individuals to be mental health promoters is an important step in preparing refugees to return.

Seventh, educate return groups regarding the role of the army in both oppressive and highly democratic societies. This was done to an important extent prior to the refugees' return to Santa María, as leaders among the returnees had carefully thought-out positions and were ready to act on their convictions. A key dimension of this education is the development of a historical perspective regarding the origin of the army's role in protecting the interests of economic elites. Another aspect is understanding how the army understands itself through its own doctrine and practice. These matters are treated in Chapters 1 and 8.

Eighth, provide returnees with long-term accompaniers during the return process. The refugee accords of October 1992 gave Guatemalan returnees the right to international accompaniment. Establishing *long-term* relationships, if not long-term residence, is critical to the return process. Santa María's record is instructive in this regard. Two people merit particular note. The first is Padre Luis Gurriarán, the priest who was so instrumental in organizing the original settlement in 1970. He continued to support the people with visits, workshops, and resources during their Mexican exile and after their return. The other person is Beatriz Manz. An anthropologist and the author of *Refugees of a Hidden War*, she first visited Santa María in 1973 and has been a key ally and an advocate for the people ever since, both in Mexico and in Guatemala.

The author's church partnership with Santa María, begun in 1987, involves twice-yearly visits, biweekly phone contact, and modest amounts of money for development projects. Finally, the work of Randall Shea with the people of Santa María while they were in Mexico and his continuing work with the schools following the return is emphasized in several chapters of this book. His work would not prosper in the absence of the highly intelligent and committed teachers living in the village, but he provides his own skill and perspective, along with contact with outside resources that have strengthened the schools. Shea has led the effort, as well, to reach out to enroll students from other communities, thereby contributing to the emerging cooperative spirit in the area.

These varieties of long-term accompaniment have assured the population that they have outside support. Further, the accompaniers have provided financial resources, key contacts, and skill to the community.

Although these suggestions are drawn from the experience of Santa María and the villages in the surrounding area, they apply, as well, to the larger return movement, in which the return to Santa María was one small part. From the author's perspective, the returnees to Santa María were well prepared for the difficult process of reintegration. The recommendations highlight the services that might have been offered sooner (human rights education) or that were not made available (education about development issues and preparation to deal more deeply with mental health problems). The relatively successful reintegration of the residents of the community demonstrated that both the returnees and those who stayed found ways to address the issues together. For this reason, the village has become a model for the country and a source for learning.

But although the refugee return movement challenged Guatemala along the lines developed in this book, and although the people in a few communities like Santa María were able to reweave the social fabric of their lives, the huge task of community and nation rebuilding remained to be tackled even after the peace accords were signed in December 1996. Guatemala was formally at peace, but, as Chapter 3 made clear, the provisions of the peace accords fell well short of establishing conditions for a just society. Further, the accords themselves became contested territory the moment they were signed, with the advantages of money, political leverage, and military force falling to the side of the powerful elite. The critical question was how far and fast the popular sectors and their solidarity allies could mobilize to give advantage to the citizen base in the country, including the indigenous majority.

Why Get Involved Now?

The final buildup and signing of documents in a peace process ending a thirty-six-year civil war is newsworthy. Pictures of President Alvaro Arzú signing the final documents for a "firm and lasting peace," standing side by side with the commanders of the revolutionary forces, were featured in major daily newspapers and on network news broadcasts in the United States. The unmistakable message was that the "Guatemalan problem" was finally solved, after all those years.

This message was put forward explicitly by U.S. special envoy to

Latin America Thomas F. McLarty in a speech to investors in mid-March 1997 in Guatemala City. His theme was that the end to Guatemala's civil war had sparked an economic revolution in the Central American region. "Where we once built stockpiles and bombs, we are now focused on stocks and bonds," he said. He went on to spell out specifics about tourism and privatization. But the tidings were clear: the Guatemalan problem was over; the opportunity phase was at hand (Snow 1997).

Ironically, many reading the articles and seeing the news were surprised that there ever was a problem in Guatemala. Unlike neighboring El Salvador and nearby Nicaragua, Guatemala never was featured as a continuing story, as an ongoing issue, in the U.S. media. Few people knew there was a civil war in which 150,000 people, most of them civilians, were killed. An article in the *Washington Post* (Snow 1997) at least told its readers that there had been a war that involved a scorched-earth policy and resulted in the Guatemalan government having "one of the worst human rights records in the hemisphere." The impact of that horrendous record, the article noted, was to scare off foreign investment. That, finally, in retrospect—in the mind of the article's author—was the crux of the Guatemalan problem.

Even among those with more than a passing interest in liberation struggles on the part of the oppressed poor around the world, the temptation after the signing of the peace accords was to turn aside from a focus on Guatemala to more current and dramatic sites. The logic was that, although Guatemala was still having serious problems, the people there must be the ones to deal with them. International solidarity was more urgently needed elsewhere.

This view misses the profound truth that this is not the time to blink or turn aside. Should the popular movement falter, should the powerful conclude that they could continue their violent coercion with impunity, all the struggle and bloodshed of the past thirty-six years would be in jeopardy. The gains written in the peace accords, however tentative, would be lost. The chance to achieve all the peace documents offered and to move beyond them to genuine redistributive justice would be gone. Momentum would shift in the other direction, with a further tearing of the social fabric.

Readers from the United States can appropriately be reminded that our country has an ugly history of undermining the poor ma-jority in Guatemala. The story of the CIA-led overthrow of the Ar-benz government in 1954 was summarized briefly in Chapter 1. The United States then trained and equipped the Guatemalan army to be an internal occupation force serving the interests of the powerful. In recent years, the CIA has been shown to be involved in the seamy underworld of Guatemalan repression, including the murders of a U.S. citizen and of a Guatemalan guerrilla commander, who was the husband of Jennifer Harbury, a U.S. citizen.

Our tax dollars, then, have through the years directly supported the forces of repression in Guatemala. We can appropriately lay claim to some responsibility for what has been done with our money in our name. We are not neutral observers.

Dwelling on that reality, however, could lead us to think of our-selves as victims of our country's duplicity, and that is not a useful outlook. The point, rather, is to understand ourselves as indirect ac-tors along the way in the repression of Guatemala who can choose now to become direct actors in enabling its people to create a more equitable society. In that framework, we can visualize this as a criti-cal transition time for the popular struggle in Guatemala as it moves to ensure that the peace accords are implemented—and beyond to more just distribution of land and resources.

What Needs to Be Done and How to Get Involved

A preliminary step in discovering how internationals can join with Guatemalans in weaving the future is to ask where, and in what ways, Guatemalans themselves have requested outside help. Returned refu-gees, for example, want internationals to accompany them by living with them in the communities where they are now living.

North American and European groups that have developed trust within Guatemala over a long period are in a position to identify groups and communities within the country that welcome specified types of help and accompaniment. These contact groups will be named and described in this section. The point is to work through groups with long-term experience and to avoid getting ahead of the initiative of the people we are attempting to help.

Those of us who live in the United States face the enormous challenge of steering this country on a path that supports genuine human rights–based democracy keyed to benefit the entire population of Guatemala. Again, the entry point is through organizations that are Guatemala focused and that maintain a constantly evolving agenda focused on aspects of U.S. policy that need to be changed. As of this writing, a major priority is to get the U.S. government to declassify all documents related to State Department and CIA involvement in Guatemala since 1950.

Six levels of involvement are described in what follows, in ascending order of their complexity and commitment. In practice, however, one can jump in at almost any point, given that others are already there who can be the mentors. The types of involvement are, in order, education, witnessing, accompaniment, advocacy, direct action, and national/international movement work.

Education. The journey here begins with self-education to a level of understanding that will make the next steps more fruitful. I vividly remember my hunger to learn when I returned from my first trip to Central America. I literally read everything I could get my hands on and went to local events featuring speakers on Central American topics. The bibliography at the end of this book points to some resources. Readers connected to churches will want to consult denominational offices for connections. National organizations working in solidarity with the popular movements in Guatemala are another excellent source for readings and contacts. These include the Network in Solidarity with the people of Guatemala (NISGUA), the National Coordinating Office for Refugees and Displaced of Guatemala (NCOORD), Guatemala Partners, Witness for Peace, and Peace Brigades International. See Appendix 1 for details on how to get in touch with these organizations.

Local universities with Latin American studies departments may also be a good point of contact for networking. If you live in an area settled by Guatemalan immigrants, you will want to contact them to hear their experiences and reasons for leaving their country. If they have participated in the struggle for justice in some arena, they may be good resources for your self-education.

In this era of electronic communication, another excellent source of information is the Internet and the World Wide Web. A good place to start is by signing on to Peacenet (call 415-561-6100 for details) and consulting the conferences that deal specifically with Guatemala. Two to start with are carnet.guatene and reg.guat.news.

On the World Wide Web, some good sites include the one from Peace Brigades International (PBI): http://www.igc.apc.org/pbi/guatemala.html. Another very helpful site is presented on behalf of Jennifer Harbury's struggle to resolve the case of her murdered husband, a former guerrilla commander. She is tireless in raising the profile of oppression in Guatemala and the need to reveal U.S. complicity in it. The site: http://www-personal.engin.umich.edu/~7Epavr/harbury. The third is put up by the University of Texas: http://lanic.utexas.edu/la/ca/guatemala/.

A good search engine for information on anything, including Guatemala, is: http://www.infoseek.com.

As one's own education gets under way, the challenge is to educate others in the various settings where we have access, including religious organizations, unions, and solidarity groups. An obvious extension of this work is to seek access in the media through letters to the editor, op ed articles, appearances on cable television, radio talk shows, newsletters, and whatever other outlets seem open to ideas and issues.

Soon, however, the need for more direct experience seems imperative.

Witnessing. The second level is to go to Guatemala to witness and experience the reality with one's own eyes and ears. I have already reported how powerful my first trip was in motivating me to become further involved. I subsequently joined a number of delegations with Witness for Peace on trips to Nicaragua and Guatemala. Other organizations that send delegations to Guatemala include Global Exchange, NISGUA, Guatemala Partners, EPICA, and the Guatemalan News and Information Bureau.

If your interest has developed individually, you may be able to recruit someone to go with you on your first trip. Another option is to join a delegation with the idea of returning home to organize others to join a later delegation. Your own enthusiasm, along with photos and other materials you bring back, can help in the recruitment.

In my case, the first trip I took, in 1985, was organized by a woman who had been to Nicaragua during the previous summer. Her commitment on her return was to organize a trip the following January. When my wife and I returned from our first trip together to Santa María, we organized a delegation from our church to go the following April, and that trip became a major stimulus for building the long-term partnership. The key dimension, in any case, is to generate a local group that serves as a base for ongoing solidarity work.

The experience of witnessing authenticates one's voice in the education of others. When I returned from my first trip, I wrote the first of a series of op ed pieces that were printed in the Boston *Globe*. They amplified my voice considerably. That, of course, was at a time when events in Central America were regularly front-page news, so the access was easier. But there are other channels, and the power of witness will make an impact.

From the witness step, the next three kinds of involvement—accompaniment, action, and advocacy—are not so much levels as options for next steps.

Accompaniment. This ties directly back to the returned refugees and their urgent desire to have internationals with them as they work for human rights–based democracy in Guatemala. This, of course, involves a more long-term commitment, typically a minimum of three months to a year or more. Readers of this book may well not have the desire or the flexibility to become accompaniers but may be in a position to suggest the role to others.

Two key organizations provide structured opportunity and training for would-be accompaniers: NCOORD and Peace Brigades International. NCOORD is particularly focused on the returned refugees. NCOORD's strategy is to recruit people to act as accompaniers, on the one hand, and as part of local U.S. support communities, on the other. Support communities serve as policy advocates, urgent action agents in response to emergencies, fund-raisers, and home base supports for specific accompaniers. Support communities may sponsor their own accompaniment person or provide support for someone recruited elsewhere in the NCOORD network. Accompaniers are carefully selected and trained for the work. One hope is that as support groups become tied in with particular Guatemalan communities, they will continue in that relationship through a series of accompaniment persons and develop a continuing, maturing partnership with the village.

Peace Brigades offers another type of opportunity to provide accompaniment. It is active in several parts of the world, including Sri Lanka, Haiti, North American indigenous communities, Columbia, and Guatemala. Its volunteers, also carefully screened and trained, provide accompaniment to individuals and groups whose leaders have received death threats. At a time of immediate and urgent danger, the accompanier may stay with the person or in the group office on a continuing basis for a time. Where the danger is ongoing but at less of a crisis level, the accompanier will check in on the endangered person daily or frequently. Another role of PBI volunteers is to offer seminars in nonviolent conflict resolution.

The Needham Congregational Church partnership with Santa María is another form of accompaniment. The original impetus for it was to bring international eyes into the area on a regular basis to deter the authorities from renewing violence in the village. Since a telephone has been installed in the village, beginning in May 1994, when the refugees returned, the church makes biweekly phone calls to check on what is happening and to assess if there is adequate accompaniment in residence. The church partnership now has its case study on the World Wide Web, which you can find at http://www.tiac.net/users/robd/guatemala.

Action. Accompaniment, of course, is a form of action, as is advocacy, which will be discussed next. Here the emphasis is on nonviolent direct action, calculated to raise the profile of Guatemala in public consciousness. Good examples are the campaigns sponsored by the Guatemala Labor Education Project (US/GLEP), which call attention to labor violations in Guatemalan factories that produce for the U.S. market. A while back the focus was on Phillips-Van Heusen shirts, which are made in Guatemalan factories that refuse to allow union organizing and threaten those who seek to introduce union activity. Another campaign involved putting pressure on Starbucks Coffee to ensure better working conditions for laborers in the fields where the coffee is grown.

The Peace and Life Committee, a U.S.-based group that parallels and works with the Campaign for Peace and Life in Guatemala, sponsors protest action to pressure the U.S. government on a variety of fronts. One recent campaign focused on the release of CIA and State Department documents that would reveal the history of U.S. involvement in Guatemalan repressive activities over the years.

Peacenet is a good source of information regarding action campaigns that local communities can get involved with.

Advocacy. Much Guatemala-focused action is keyed to advocacy around specific campaigns and issues. The emphasis in this section is on getting Congress to effect legislation. The goal is to develop strong connections with congressional aides working with senators and representatives on foreign policy, specifically Latin American, issues. A woman living in my town developed a very strong link with a key aide to Joe Moakley, a Democratic representative from Massachusetts, and she helped me build on that relationship, which gave me a strong tie as well. Her focus wasn't Guatemala as such, but I got access to discuss that issue with Representative Moakley through her good work. Aggressive networking in your area may provide similar ready access.

The most effective advocacy work I am aware of was not Guatemala-related at all but illustrates the power of citizen advocacy when it is well organized. The Piedmont Peace Project in North Carolina began work in a conservative political climate with a progressive agenda of empowering poor people in the area. By developing a broadly based network of very locally organized groups, it created an organizational base that convinced an initially conservative congressperson to embrace a progressive agenda.

The point is to start very locally and as effectively as possible in educating congressional representatives and senators over the long haul with clearly thought-out issue-oriented presentations. NISGUA puts out a legislative update on issues related to Guatemala that is very helpful to legislators. Witness for Peace is also focused on U.S. policy issues and is a good source of advocacy information.

National/international movement building. Much more progressive activity, including action on Guatemalan issues, goes on in this country than we are aware of because the national media do not cover much solidarity work. Therefore, those of us involved need to be aggressive in seeking out what is already going on so we can be effective in adding to the strength of national efforts. Newsletters of national organizations, such as Peace Brigades, Guatemala Partners, the Guatemala News and Information Bureau, Witness for Peace, NCOORD, and NISGUA, can be particularly helpful here.

Work at the national level is clearly an advanced level of involvement. But it is critical to have some version of a larger vision that is massive enough to make a liberating impact on the poor majority in Guatemala who have been the focus of this book. Effective action keyed to enabling human rights–based democracy both there and here needs to begin locally, but clearly it cannot end there. Creeks need to flow to streams to rivers to the sea change that is required.

Beyond Guatemala lies the need to build the movement with activists working for a just El Salvador, a just Nicaragua, and on to the more encompassing issues that embrace Latin America and the Third World. At that level, we face again the challenge of the global economy. There the transnational corporations work in the class interests of the economic elites, including the rich of Guatemala. We may not be ready to deal with that level of power as we take the first steps toward involvement, but we do well to keep it in our perspective. An important way to develop countervailing pressure on transnational corporations is for leaders of the popular movements in particular countries to join their work with counterparts in other countries. Having visited Haiti and met with popular movement leaders there, I am conscious of how important it is for organizers there to be working not only with movement leaders in Guatemala but also with African American and Latina/o leaders from the cities of North America.

The movement, then, is from education and analysis to witnessing with one's own eyes and ears on to organizing to build the base for accompaniment, action, and big-league advocacy. From there, the next step is to the expansion of national and international networks of progressives in a common struggle for a global economy rooted in human rights and economic democracy that expresses the voice and action of the majority of the world's people.

A recent U.N. publication noted that one-fifth of the world's people live on less than a dollar a day. The publication featured a graphic depiction of the distribution of wealth in the world. It showed a champagne glass with a large cup area, representing the fact that the upper 20 percent of the world's people have 83.7 percent of the world's wealth. But there was no base on the glass, a stark representation of the fact that the bottom 60 percent of the world's people have just 6.4 percent of its wealth (United Nations 1992, inside front cover).

In such a world, there is no justice, and there can be no genuine peace or human rights–based democracy. While so many are in poverty and live under repression, all of us are diminished. We live on the same lifeboat.

But what is overwhelming on the grand scale is richly human and emotionally engaging in particular places. Returned refugees are reweaving their lives with those who stayed in Santa María Tzejá. There, parents are working to feed, clothe, and house themselves and their children and to develop their community as a whole. There, education promoters serve not only the children and youth of the community but students from neighboring communities. There, human rights promoters hold workshops to raise the awareness of their fellow villagers to their lives as dignified, whole human beings. There, people struggle with nightmares and physical symptoms, open wounds from the constant trauma of the early 1980s, and think about how to rebury the massacred in a way that will bring maximum healing to the community. There, they confront fear on a daily basis regarding how to face down an army that would rather control than liberate them.

We who are diminished by their poverty and the injustice that surrounds them can be enriched by joining them in a struggle for liberation for them and for us. In joining that struggle, or one like it, we will have our eyes opened to the deepening poverty and injustice that exist a few short minutes from our homes. We will widen our vision to see that the same system that is impoverishing the poor in Guatemala is widening the ranks of the poor in North America. The challenge is to reweave the torn—there and here.

U.S. Groups Providing Resources on Guatemala and Support for the Peace Process

Campaign for Peace and Life in Guatemala
1830 Connecticut Ave. NW
Washington, D.C. 20009
(202) 462-3935
Ecumenical religious coalition that supports progressive social change in Guatemala; active in the campaign to declassify U.S. government documents relating to human rights abuses in Guatemala.

Ecumenical Program on Central America (EPICA)
1470 Irving St. NW
Washington, DC 20010
(202) 332-0292
E-mail: epica@igc.apc.org
Informs and mobilizes North Americans on hemispheric issues of social justice and self-determination; publishes a quarterly journal, *Challenge: Faith and Action in the Americas*.

Guatemala News and Information Bureau (GNIB)
P.O. Box 28594
Oakland, CA 94604
(510) 835-0810
E-mail: gnib@igc.apc.org
Northern California group that supports the Guatemalan popular movement; maintains an extensive library of resources on Guatemala; publishes the quarterly *Report on Guatemala* and the monthly *Update on Guatemala*.

Guatemala Partners
1830 Connecticut Ave. NW
Washington, DC 20009
(202) 783-1123
E-mail: manos@igc.apc.org
Raises funds for community development projects, focusing on four main areas: women; health; refugees and displaced; environmental and cultural preservation.

Guatemalan Human Rights Commission / USA
3321 12th St. NE
Washington, DC 20017
(202) 529-6599
E-mail: ghrc@igc.apc.org
Monitors and reports on Guatemala's human rights situation; supports the legal
campaigns of Jennifer Harbury and Dianna Ortiz; posts emergency human rights alerts.

National Coordinating Office on Refugees and Displaced of Guatemala (NCOORD)
1830 Connecticut Ave. NW
Washington, DC 20009
(202) 265-8713
E-mail: ncoord@igc.apc.org
Coordinates U.S. support for Guatemalan refugees and return communities through
education, advocacy, and direct accompaniment projects. Sponsors the Guatemalan
Accompaniment Project (GAP).

Network in Solidarity with the People of Guatemala (NISGUA)
1830 Connecticut Ave. NW
Washington, DC 20009
(202) 223-6474
E-mail: nisgua@igc.apc.org
National network of groups that sponsors U.S. speaking tours of Guatemalan activists;
raises funds for popular movement groups; coordinates policy advocacy in Washington,
D.C.; and operates a human rights rapid-response network.

Peace Brigades International
2642 College Ave.
Berkeley, CA 94704
(510) 540-0749
E-mail: pbiusa@igc.apc.org
International group that sends volunteers to live in Guatemala, accompanying human
rights/social change advocates and threatened communities.

U.S.-Guatemala Labor Education Project (US/GLEP)
P.O. Box 268–290
Chicago, IL 60626
(773) 262-6502
E-mail: usglep@igc.apc.org
Supports labor union organizing in Guatemala through educational and activist
campaigns; lobbies Congress on Guatemalan trade issues; builds ties between U.S.
and Guatemalan workers.

Chronology of Guatemalan History

1524	Spanish conquest; beginning of colonial era.
1821	Independence from Spain.
1871	Dictatorship of Gen. Justo Rufino Barrios; "liberal reforms" in the modernization of agriculture and the introduction of coffee on a big scale; disestablishment of the Catholic church; church and indigenous lands taken for the cultivation of coffee.
1898	Dictatorship of Estrada Cabrera.
1901	United Fruit Company (UFCo) arrives in Guatemala.
1920	Cabrera dictatorship overthrown; United States intervenes militarily.
1931	Dictatorship of Jorge Ubico; repression of leftists and unions.
1944	Ubico overthrown in military coup; civilian-military uprising subsequently ousts military junta and sponsors elections.
1945	Juan José Arévalo elected president; democratic constitution promulgated.
1947	New labor code establishes basic workers' rights.
1950	Jacobo Arbenz elected president.
1952	Agrarian Reform Law passed.
1953	Arbenz government distributes former United Fruit land to 100,000 campesino families.
1954	Arbenz overthrown in CIA-organized "Liberation" and Castillo Armas takes power; land reform reversed and popular organizations crushed.
1957	Castillo Armas assassinated.
1958	Conservative Gen. Miguel Ydígoras Fuentes elected president.
1960	Major military uprising against Ydígoras suppressed; some participants go into hiding.
1961	Massive student and labor demonstrations, formation of MR-13 and Rebel Armed Forces (FAR), and beginning of guerrilla insurgency.

Sources: Fried et. al. 1983; Barry 1992; Jonas 1991; Loeb and Alvarado 1996.

1963	Army deposes Ydígoras and installs the defense minister, Col. Alfredo Enríque Peralta Azurdia, as president.
1966	Julio Cesar Méndez Montenegro elected president. Military dominates the government.
1966–68	United States sends Green Berets, finances and directs counterinsurgency campaign led by Col. Carlos Arana Osorio; founding of MANO Blanca and other death squads; by 1970, eight thousand unarmed civilians killed by security forces.
1970	Col. Arana elected president. State of siege imposed; repression intensifies.
1971	Formation of ORPA (Organization of People in Arms) guerrilla group.
1972	Entry of EGP (Guerrilla Army of the Poor) guerrillas into the Ixcán region of northern Guatemala.
1974	Gen. Kjell Laugerud becomes president, through electoral fraud.
1975	Guerrilla activities resume.
1976	Powerful earthquake kills twenty-two thousand. Formation of National Committee of Trade Union Unity (CNUS); increased popular organizing.
1977	Massive protest march by mineworkers from Ixtahuacán to Guatemala City. Met by 100,000 supporters in Guatemala City.
1978	Gen. Romeo Lucas García becomes president through electoral fraud. Formation of Committee of Peasant Unity (CUC). Massacre of Maya indigenous at Panzós. United States bans arms sales to Guatemalan government
1979	ORPA guerrillas launch first military operation.
1980	Government massacre and burning of the Spanish embassy; Spain breaks diplomatic relations; nearly eighty thousand farm workers strike, forcing increase in the minimum wage. Great increase in guerrilla activity in highlands.
1981	Beginning of army counteroffensive, involving numerous massacres and destruction of more than four hundred indigenous villages by 1983.
1982	Formation of Guatemalan National Revolutionary Unity (URNG) by EGP, ORPA, FAR, and PGT nucleus. Gen. Angel Aníbal Guevara "wins" presidency through fraudulent election, but discontented army officers led by Gen. Efraín Ríos Montt seize power in coup; Ríos Montt becomes president; counterinsurgency campaign escalates, including scorched-earth drive in the Ixcán; civil patrols formed.

1983   United States resumes military sales to Guatemala. Gen. Oscar Mejía Victores seizes power in military coup; counterinsurgency war continues.

1984   Constituent Assembly draws up new constitution. Formation of Mutual Support Group (GAM) of the relatives of the disappeared.

1985   Official U.S. economic and military aid resumed. Christian Democrat Vinicio Cerezo wins presidency in national election.

1986   Cerezo assumes presidency in January.

1987   Esquipulas II, Central American Peace Accords, signed. Army begins "Year's End" counterinsurgency offensive, which fails in its goal to eliminate the guerrillas.

1988   Abortive military coup attempt by rightist civilians and military officers, leading Cerezo to back down on his commitments to unions and other popular groups.

1989   Another failed coup attempt.

1990   Beginning of "Dialogue" process of discussions between URNG and political and social sectors. Presidential election, first round. Massacre at Santiago Atitlán.

1991   Jorge Serrano wins runoff election.

1992   Signing of accords on the return of refugees from Mexico to Guatemala, between Permanent Commissions and the Guatemalan government.

1993   First massive refugee return to Victoria, 20 de enero (20th of January). President Serrano suspends constitution, Congress, and the courts and announces rule by decree. In June, Congress selects Ramiro de León Carpio, former human rights ombudsman, as president.

1994   United Nations becomes mediator of the Guatemalan peace process.

1995   National elections in November, won by Alvaro Arzú of the National Advancement Party (PAN). President Arzú assumes office in January.

1996   Signing of "firm and lasting peace" accords on December 29, ending thirty-six years of civil war.

Chronology of the
Guatemalan Peace Process

April 26, 1991	Procedures for the Search for Peace by Political Means, outlines plan for the peace talks and order in which topics will be discussed
July 25, 1991	Framework Accord on Democratization, statement of overall goals
January 10, 1994	Framework Accord for the Renewal of the Negotiating Process, provides for United Nations moderation of talks and verification of agreements; creates the Assembly of Civil Society (ASC); creates the "Group of Friends" countries to nurture the peace process: Mexico, Venezuela, Colombia, Spain, Norway, and the United States.
March 29, 1994	Comprehensive Accord on Human Rights; Accord on Calendarization
June 17, 1994	Accord for the Resettlement of Populations Uprooted by the Armed Conflict
June 23, 1994	Accord on Establishing a Commission for the Historical Clarification of Human Rights Violations and Violent Acts Causing Suffering in the Guatemalan Population
March 31, 1995	Accord on the Rights and Identity of Indigenous Peoples
May 6, 1996	Accord on Socioeconomic Aspects and the Agrarian Situation
September 19, 1996	Accord on Strengthening Civil Power and the Role of the Army in a Democratic Society
December 4, 1996	Definitive Cease-Fire Accord
December 7, 1996	Accord on Constitutional and Electoral Systems Reforms
December 12, 1996	Accord on the Incorporation of the URNG into Society
December 18, 1996	Passage of the Law of National Reconciliation
December 29, 1996	Accord on a Firm and Lasting Peace

Sources: Loeb and Alvarado 1996; URNG 1995; and Guatemala Team Report 1997.

Acronyms

ARAP-KSI	Regional Association of Landholders of the Ixcán
ASC	Assembly of Civil Society
CACIF	Chamber of Agricultural, Commercial, Industrial, and Financial Associations
CEAR	Special Commission for the Assistance of Refugees and Repatriates (Guatemala)
CECI	Canadian Center for International Studies and Cooperation
CIA	U.S. Central Intelligence Agency
CIREFCA	International Conference on Refugees, Repatriates and Displaced of Central America
CNOC	National Coordination of Campesino Organizations
COINDE	Council of Development Institutions
COMAR	Mexican Commission for Help with Refugees
COPMAGUA	Coordinator of Maya Peoples Organizations
CORDHI	Regional Human Rights Alliance of the Ixcán
CPR	Communities of Population in Resistance
CUC	Campesino Unity Committee
FIS	Social Investment Fund
FDNG	Democratic Front for a New Guatemala
IMF	International Monetary Fund
INTA	Institute of Agrarian Transformation
MINUGUA	United Nations Mission to Guatemala
NCOORD	National Coordinating Office on Refugees, Returnees, and Displaced of Guatemala
NISGUA	Network in Solidarity with the People of Guatemala
OCADHI	Catholic Office for Human Rights in the Ixcán
OPODEDHGUA	Popular Organization for the Defense of Human Rights in Guatemala
ORPA	Organization of People under Arms
PAN	National Advancement Party

PRODERE	Development Program for Displaced, Refugees, and Repatriates in Central America
PRODESSA	Santiago Development Project
REMHI	Recovery of Historical Memory
SAPs	Structural Adjustment Programs
UASP	Labor and Popular Action Unity
UNHCR	United Nations High Commission for Refugees
URNG	Guatemalan National Revolutionary Unity
USAID	U.S. Agency for International Development
WTO	World Trade Organization

Notes

Introduction

1. For information on the CPRs in Ixcán, see Garst 1993, 28–31. See also Manz 1994, 202–8, and Manuel 1994, 85–93.

2. For numbers on who fled and the original settlements in Mexico, see Manz 1988a, chap. 6.

3. They were "historic" in the sense of being refugee controlled for the first time anywhere. National Coordinating Office on Refugees and Displaced of Guatemala newsletter, "Special Issue: The Permanent Commissions." The unnamed author notes, "According to the United Nations High Commission for Refugees (UNHCR), this was the first time a direct accord setting out the conditions of return had been negotiated by the refugees themselves with the government of the country from which they fled" (1).

4. Various sources contain different figures regarding the levels of poverty in Guatemala. Jonas 1991 consistently refers to the figure 87 percent. Barry 1992 indicates a range of 80 to 87 percent, based on 1990 figures, citing a range of sources, including the United Nations. Barry notes, "Poverty statistics vary according to agency, but all surveys show that poverty has mushroomed since 1980 and that approximately four out of every five Guatemalans live below the poverty line" (95).

5. For a general description of the colonization of the Ixcán, see Garst 1993, 15–22.

6. The author was present for that repatriation. Informal interviews took place in subsequent years.

Chapter One

1. Notes from the briefing taken by the author.

2. Electronic mail, Guatemalan news agency Cerigua, December 23, 1996.

3. Paula Worby, currently working with the United Nations High Commission for Refugees, points out the source of the figure of 440 villages destroyed by the army. "In two army publications, they mentioned that more than 400,

in one case, and 440 in another, had been destroyed, but they refer to it in the context of damage that the subversives had done. But then a 1985 WOLA [Washington Office on Latin America] document quoted the figure with its army source and everyone else began to misquote it as the army's own account of the villages the army itself had destroyed." The exact number of villages destroyed is not the issue. The magnitude of the numbers the army cited are suggestive of the extent of the destruction, and there is compelling evidence that the army was the destroyer. See Falla 1994, with its overwhelming evidence of army authorship of destroyed villages.

4. Guatemalan Church in Exile 1989. On the beans and bullets theme, see also Carmack 1988, 63.

5. This and the following testimonies are taken from the diaries of Clark and Kay Taylor recorded during various visits to the village.

6. Testimony at the site of the burial, given to a church delegation in August 1996.

7. See, for example, Schlesinger and Kinzer 1983; Gleijeses 1991; and Immerman 1984. A good description of the period leading up to the 1944 revolution is in Dosal 1993.

8. McClintock 1985, 54. See also Institute of Policy Studies, "Behind Guatemala's Military Power," in Fried et al. 1983, 128; and Aguilera Peralta 1983, 118–19.

9. See Hinkelammert 1991 for a powerful development of this theme.

10. Testimony shared with Clark and Kay Taylor, July 1994 .

Chapter Two

1. For a detailed description and analysis of the refugee experience in Mexico, see Manz 1988a.

Chapter Three

1. See also Ciborsky and Carroll 1997, 5, and Swedish 1996a, 14, regarding the role of international pressure.

2. See also Levinson-Estrada 1994 for a fuller account.

3. Regarding neoliberalism, see, for example, Rosen 1995, 84–94.

Chapter Four

1. By sheer chance, I was in the audience. Our delegation arrived about a half hour after the U.N. group had entered the village. The quote here is from my notes at the time.

2. Chance encounters with the man in Nueva Trinitaria and a representative of the nine families provided me with this information. Information regarding the Protestant pastor was provided by Paula Worby in a June 1997 conversation.

3. The meeting with the education supervisor took place in July 1994, with the author in attendance.

4. Meetings dealing with this issue took place in June 1995, when the author was in the village.

Chapter Five

1. For an important discussion of the role of the state in neoliberalism, see Hinkelammert 1994, 12–27.

2. This quote is from notes taken at the meeting by Randall Shea.

Chapter Six

1. The Guatemalan constitution can be read in Spanish on the World Wide Web at: http://www.pronet.net.gt/leyes/demo0001/constitu.htm.

Chapter Eight

1. Figures are from the Ecumenical Program on Central America and the Caribbean and the Center for Human Rights Legal Action.

Chapter Nine

1. Dan Long is the World Council of Churches' representative in Guatemala and a member of the international mediating body that helped determine conditions for the returns.

Bibliography

Aguilera Peralta, Gabriel. 1983. "The Militarization of the Guatemalan State." In Jonathan L. Fried et al., eds., *Guatemala in Rebellion: Unfinished History*, 114–22. New York: Grove Press.

Barry, Tom. 1992. *Inside Guatemala: The Essential Guide to Its Politics, Economy, Society, and Environment.* Albuquerque, N.M.: Inter-Hemispheric Education and Resource Center.

———. 1995. "Guatemala: A Test for Democratization." *Democracy Backgrounder* (electronic ed.; occasional paper). Albuquerque, N.M.: Inter-Hemispheric Education and Resource Center.

Becker, David. 1994. "Trauma, Duelo e Identidad: Una Reflexión Conceptual." In David Becker, Germán Morales, and María Inés Aguilar, eds., *Trauma Psicosocial y Adolescentes Latinoamericanos: Formas de Acción Grupal.* Santiago, Chile: Instituto Latinoamericano de Salud Mental y Derechos Humanos.

Carmack, Robert. 1988. "The Story of Santa Cruz Quiché." In Robert Carmack, ed., *The Harvest of Violence: The Guatemala Crisis*, 39–69 Norman: University of Oklahoma Press.

Cerigua News Agency. 1996. "Interview with Benedictus Lucas." Dec. 23.

———. 1997a. "Army Crimes Continue." *Cerigua Weekly Briefs*, March 19 (electronic ed.).

———. 1997b. "Defensoría Maya Denuncia Militarización." *Cerigua Weekly Briefs*, Jan. 25 (electronic ed.).

———. 1997c. "Militares Podrian Participar en Policia Nacional Civil." *Cerigua Weekly Briefs*, Feb. 17 (electronic ed.).

———. 1997d. "Por Violar los Acuerdos de Paz, el CERJ Rechazo Patrullajes del Ejercito." *Cerigua Weekly Briefs*, April 12 (electronic ed.).

———. 1997e. "Troops Sent into Streets to Control Crime." *Cerigua Weekly Briefs*, April 12 (electronic ed.).

Chomsky, Noam. 1996. "From Containment to Rollback: Will Civilization Die?" *Z Magazine*, June, 22–31.

Ciborski, Marian, and David Carroll. 1997. *Making Peace in Guatemala.* Washington, D.C.: Witness for Peace.

Conde, Daniel. 1983. "Guatemalan Refugees in Mexico." *Cultural Survival Quarterly*, Winter, 49–53.

Defensoría Maya. 1997. "Banda Militar en el Deparemento del Quiché Conformada por Elementos del Ejercito; Gran Desestabilización al Proceso de Paz." June 28 (electronic bulletin).

Dosal, Paul J. 1993. *Doing Business with Dictators: A Political History of United Fruit in Guatemala, 1899–1944*. Wilmington, Del.: Scholarly Resources.

Falla, Ricardo. 1994. *Massacres in the Jungle: Ixcán, Guatemala, 1975–1982*. Boulder, Colo.: Westview Press.

Freire, Paulo. 1970. *Pedagogy of the Oppressed*. New York: Continuum Press.

Fried, Jonathan, et al., eds. 1983. *Guatemala in Rebellion: Unfinished History*. New York: Grove Press.

Galeano, Eduardo. 1982. *Days of Love & War*. New York: Monthly Review Press.

Garoz, Byron. 1996. *CIREFCA y la Atención al Desarraigo en Centroamerica*. Guatemala City: COINDE.

Garst, Rachel. 1993. *Ixcán: Colonización, Desarraigo y Condiciones de Retorno*. Guatemala City: COINDE.

Ghiglia, José Alberto. 1997. "El Trabajo de Derechos Humanos en Ixcán (Desde 1993–1996) a Partir de la Etica Cristiana." Master's thesis, Randival Landivar University.

Gleijeses, Piero. 1991. *Shattered Hope: The Guatemalan Revolution and the United States, 1945–1954*. Princeton, N.J.: Princeton University Press.

Guatemalan Church in Exile. 1989. *Guatemala: Security, Development, and Democracy*.

Guatemala Human Rights Commission/USA. 1996. "Military Training Continues Despite Peace Accord." *Guatemala Human Rights Update* no. 2. Washington, D.C.

Guatemala News and Information Bureau. 1997a. *Update on Guatemala*. Oakland, Calif. April.

———. 1997b. *Update on Guatemala*. Oakland, Calif. Aug.

Guatemala Team Report. 1997. "The End of the Armed Conflict." *Peace Brigades International Project Bulletin*, Feb.

Gurriarán, Luis. 1993. "The History of Santa María Tzejá." Interview with Padre Luis. Trans. Kay Taylor. Mimeo.

Handy, Jim. 1984. *Gift of the Devil: A History of Guatemala*. Boston: South End Press.

Hernandez Pico, Juan, S. J. 1997. "Peace Accords: Return of the Quetzal." *Envío*, Feb.-March, 14–21.

Hernandez, Raón. 1997. "Entrevista con Gral. Julio Balconi Turcios." *Prense Libre*, June 15 (electronic ed.).

Hinkelammert, Franz. 1991. *Sacrificios Humanos y Sociedad Occidental.* San José, Costa Rica: DEI.

————. 1994. "Our Project for the New Society in Latin America: The Regulating Role of the State and Problems of Self-Regulation in the Market." In Susanne Jonas and Edward McCaughan, eds., *Latin America Faces the Twenty-First Century,* 12–17. Boulder, Colo.: Westview Press.

Immerman, Richard H. 1984. *The CIA in Guatemala.* Austin: University of Texas Press.

Interiano, Elder. 1996. "Opinión." *Prense Libre,* Nov. 25 (electronic ed.).

Jeffrey, Paul. 1996. "Guatemala: False Peace at Hand?" *Latinamerica Press,* Dec. 5, 8.

————. 1997. "Peace Will Face Many Challenges." *Latinamerica Press,* Jan. 16, 2.

Jonas, Susanne. 1991. *The Battle for Guatemala: Rebels, Death Squads, and U.S. Power.* Boulder, Colo.: Westview Press.

————. 1997. "The Peace Accords: An End and a Beginning." *NACLA Report on the Americas,* May-June, 6–10.

Khor, Martin. 1996. "Globalization Needs Guidance at the International Level." *Third World Economics* (Malaysia), May 1–15, 4.

Levinson-Estrada, Deborah. 1994. *Trade Unionists against Terror: Guatemala City, 1954–1985.* Chapel Hill: University of North Carolina Press.

Lira, Elizabeth, and María Isabel Castillo. 1991. *Psicología de la Amenaza Política y del Miedo.* Santiago, Chile: Instituto Latinoamericano de Salud Mental y Derechos Humanos.

Loeb, David, and Bernardo Alvarado. 1996. *Guatemala: The Long Road to Peace.* San Fransisco: Global Exchange.

Long, Dan. 1997a. *Situation Report #47.* Guatemala City: World Council of Churches. May 27.

————. 1997b. *Situation Report #50.* Guatemala City: World Council of Churches. Nov. 26.

Loveman, Brian. 1998. *For the Patria: Politics and the Armed Forces in Latin America.* Wilmington, Del.: Scholarly Resources.

Manuel, Ann. 1994. *Human Rights in Guatemala during President De León Carpio's First Year.* New York: Human Rights Watch/Americas.

Manz, Beatriz. 1988a. *Refugees of a Hidden War.* Albany, N.Y.: SUNY Press.

————. 1988b. "The Transformation of La Experanza, an Ixcán Village." In Robert A. Carmack, ed., *Harvest of Violence: The Guatemala Crisis,* 70–89. Norman: University of Oklahoma Press.

————. 1994. "Epilogue." In Ricardo Falla, *Massacres in the Jungle,* 191–211. Boulder, Colo.: Westview Press.

McClintock, Michael. 1985. *The American Connection,* vol. 2, *State Terror and Popular Resistance in Guatemala.* London: Zed Books.

Morrissey, James. 1978. "A Missionary Directed Resettlement Project among the Highland Maya of Western Guatemala." Ph.D. diss., Stanford University.

NCOORD. 1996. "The Permanent Commissions." *NCOORD Newsletter*, Special Issue, July.

———. 1997. "Repatriations/Returns from 1984–1996." *NCOORD Newsletter*, March-April.

NISGUA. 1996. "Military Accord Signed." *Solidarity Update*, Oct., 1–2.

———. 1997. "The Post War Era Begins." *Solidarity Update*, March, 1–2.

Oficina Coordinadora, Conferencia Episcopal de Guatemala. 1994. *Hacia un Retorno con Dignidad y Seguridad.* Guatemala City.

O'Kane, Patricia. 1997. "ICVA/GRICAR Report No. 30." Guatemala City. Feb. 6.

Peace Brigades International. 1977. *Bulletin,* Feb.

Popkin, Margaret. 1996. *Civil Patrols and Their Legacy.* Washington, D.C.: Robert F. Kennedy Memorial Center for Human Rights.

Rader, Jennifer. 1997. "Un Paso Adelante: Human Rights Education and the Strengthening of Civil Society in Ixcán, Guatemala." Master's thesis, University of California, Berkeley.

Rosen, Fred. 1995. "Venezuela: The Temperature Rises in the Crucible of Reform." In Fred Rosen and Deidre McFadyen, eds., *Free Trade and Economic Restructuring in Latin America*, 84–94. New York: Monthly Review Press.

Schirmer, Jennifer. 1991. "The Guatemalan Military Project: An Interview with Gen. Héctor Gramajo." *Harvard International Review*, Spring, 10–13.

Schlesinger, Stephen, and Steven Kinzer. 1983. *Bitter Fruit.* New York: Doubleday.

Snow, Anita. 1997. "U.S. Says Guatemala Recovering." *Washington Post*, March 13.

Swedish, Margaret. 1996a. "Guatemala: After Serious Glitch, Peace Talks Head toward Solution." *Central America/Mexico Report* 16, Dec., 14.

———. 1996b. "Will an Accord Bring Peace?" *Central America/Mexico Report* 16, Dec. 5, 14.

———. 1997. "Guatemala: Constructing the Peace." *Central America/Mexico Report* 17, Feb. 1, 8–9.

Timerman, Jacobo. 1987. *Chile: Death in the South.* New York: Vintage Books.

Tovar-Siebentritt, Gretta. 1996. *Guatemala: Return to Violence: Refugees, Civil Patrollers, and Impunity.* New York: Human Rights Watch/Americas.

United Nations. 1992. *Human Development Report.* New York.

URNG. 1995. *Guatemala: Negociaciones de Paz—Contenido do los Acuerdos Firmados por el Gobierno/Ejércity y la URNG.* Mexico City.

Index

223